The Political Economy
of U.S. Import Policy

The Political Economy
of U.S. Import Policy

Robert E. Baldwin

The MIT Press
Cambridge, Massachusetts
London, England

This book was set in Palatino by Achorn Graphic Services, Inc., and printed and bound by Halliday Lithograph in the United States of America.

Library of Congress Cataloging in Publication Data

Baldwin, Robert E.
  The political economy of U.S. import policy.

  Bibliography: p.
  Includes index.
  1. United States—Commercial policy.   I. Title.
II. Title: Political economy of US import policy.
HF1455.B26   1985   382'.5'0973   85-18140
ISBN 0-262-02232-X

To Janice

Contents

Preface

This study is based on the belief that international economists need to devote more attention to the political economy of trade policies in order to understand better how import and export policies are determined and to be more helpful in assisting public officials in their decision making on trade issues. Economists have long implicitly assumed that the concern for national economic welfare underlying most of their policy analyses is also the most important motivating force for elected officials. Yet judging by a comparison of the policy implications of the analyses by international economists with the trade policies actually implemented by democratic governments, it seems evident that the goals of public officials have included much more than the maximization of national economic welfare.

To try to understand better just how public officials go about making policy decisions, some economists have begun to apply the same methods they use in analyzing economic behavior in the private marketplace to analyze behavior in the political marketplace. This study utilizes this approach. Beginning with a simple, short-run self-interest public choice model, the analytical framework is further developed by introducing political behavior based on long-run self-interest as well as on social concerns and ethical standards. On the basis of this framework, various hypotheses concerning trade policy behavior by individuals and groups in the private sector and individuals and agencies in the public sector are formulated and tested statistically or by analyzing particular trade policy events.

For those closely involved with trade ‚policy matters, many of the hypotheses tested statistically will seem obvious and the test results unsurprising. These individuals know the validity of the hypotheses from their personal experience. The purpose here, however, is to establish the relationships between various economic and political factors and trade policies in a more rigorous manner than individual experience usually yields and to provide more information about the relative importance of different factors. There are also several instances in which the conventional wisdom based on personal experience is not supported by statistical analysis. One can never be sure just which parts of conventional trade policy wisdom require reconsideration until all are tested.

A secondary purpose of the study is to outline the roles of three parts of the federal government in shaping U.S. trade policy—namely, the Congress, the International Trade Commission, and the Executive Branch—and to describe the involvement of each in some significant trade policy issues of recent years. Chapters 2, 3, and 4 deal with these bodies, explaining their functions, how they have changed over the years, and the motivations of their members with regard to import issues. This makes for some repetition but enables each of the three chapters to stand as a unit that can be read separately.

I am very grateful to the World Bank for providing financial support as well as office and secretarial facilities in the Bank from August 1978 to July 1979, when I undertook much of the research for the study. I am especially appreciative of the support and encouragement received from Helen Hughes, in whose department at the Bank I was housed. Bela Balassa was also most helpful in formulating the nature of the study. Financial assistance from the Graduate School at the University of Wisconsin-Madison and from the National Bureau of Economic Research, which enabled me to complete the study, is also gratefully acknowledged.

Parts of the study have been presented at a number of conferences and seminars. Among the very valuable comments received on these occasions, as well as from persons who had read preliminary versions of the study, were those from Kym Anderson, C. Fred Bergsten, Jagdish Bhagwati, Jeurgen Donges, J. Michael Finger, Isaiah Frank, Theodore Gates, Gerald Helleiner, Irving Kravis, Ian Little, Stephen Magee, Rachel McCulloch, John Odell, J. David Richardson, Edward Ray, Walter Salant, T. N. Srinivasan, Jean Waelbroeck, and Stanislaw Wellisz.

I should like to express my gratitude to R. Spence Hilton, who as my research assistant throughout most of the study not only carried out much of the statistical analysis but provided valuable analytical advice; to Kris Hallberg and Michael Anderson, who also provided excellent research assistance; and to my daughter, Nancy, who searched out and collected much of the information on congressional actions. Nancy Klatt has not only done an excellent job in typing the manuscript but has been very helpful with editorial assistance.

The Political Economy
of U.S. Import Policy

1   The Political Economy of Protectionism

1.1 Introduction

The objective of this study is to add to our knowledge concerning the manner in which U.S. import policies are determined. Although economic historians have often analyzed the economic and political factors that shape U.S. international trade policies, trade economists have generally not devoted much attention to this topic.[1] They have instead usually taken as given the existence of various trade policies, such as free trade or import protection, and then analyzed the economic efficiency and redistributive implications of these policies. The major conclusion from this positive analysis is that import protection reduces a country's real income level unless the country possesses enough monopoly power to improve its terms of trade sufficiently to offset the welfare losses to consumers that result from the higher prices of the protected products.[2] Economists have further shown that if society wishes to modify the domestic distribution of income resulting from the free market mechanism, there are less distorting means of accomplishing this goal than by introducing barriers to international trade.

Most economists believe that explaining how and why the government maintains import restrictions is a subject more appropriate for study by political scientists and sociologists than by economists.[3] Within the last decade, however, this attitude has changed, and a number of studies dealing with the political economy of protectionism have been undertaken by trade economists. This greater interest in trying to explain such matters as interindustry differences in levels of protection and the difference in behavior between the Congress and the president in the face of protectionist pressures is only one indication of the growing interest by economists in the theory of public choice, a subject that Mueller (1976) defines as the application of economics to political science.[4]

According to Mueller, public choice theory developed as a separate field in the 1950s and 1960s, when some economists began to inquire whether government policies required to correct for those situations where the free market fails to allocate economic resources efficiently (such as the existence of technological externalities or monopoly power) would in fact be adopted under the political processes characterizing modern industrial democracies. In addition, they began to ask why and how various government policies were introduced that, instead of correcting economic distortions, created them as a by-product of income redistribution and other social objectives. An example of this latter situation, as the early writers on public choice noted, is the use of tariffs and other trade-restricting measures to protect particular economic interests from the competitive consequences of imports.

Public choice theory serves as the basic analytical framework for this study of U.S. import policies. The theory itself is based on the assumption that all individuals' welfare depends only on the goods and services a person consumes directly. It will, however, be modified from this pure version that stresses short-run economic self-interest as the motivating force of the participants in political decisions. In particular, long-run self-interest and interpersonal considerations and social concerns are also introduced as motivating factors for voters and their political leaders. This chapter outlines the broad analytical framework to be followed, first by presenting the basic theory and then introducing certain modifications suggested by various authors. From this analysis a number of general hypotheses can be derived that in later chapters will be tested empirically or illustrated with recent trade policy events.

At the outset of a study of U.S. import policies, it is important to emphasize that not only are there many different forms of import policies but that public decisions affecting the volume and composition of imports are made in many different parts of the U.S. government. The general policy framework is established by the Congress together with the president in the form of legislation that provides the president with the authority to carry out various trade-related programs and sets forth broad guidelines to be followed in doing so. Decisions concerning levels of import protection for particular sectors are usually made by various agencies within the executive branch that implement this general legislation. The International Trade Commission (ITC), an independent, quasi-judicial agency, makes recommendations to the president concerning whether import relief should be granted to an industry because of an injurious increase in imports. The Office of the United States Trade Representative (USTR), which is part of the Executive Office of the President, plays the leadership role in determining the extent of the cuts in industry tariff levels to be made in multilateral trade negotiations. Still another key agency is the Department of Commerce, which deals with requests for import protection from industries on grounds of dumping, subsidization, and national security.

A division of trade policy authority that assigns the determination of the general policy framework to the Congress and the implementation of the broad guidelines set
forth by this body to different agencies within the executive branch is, however, overly simplified. For example,
through its ability to publicize the problems of particular
industries in public hearings and by threatening to enact
legislation that provides protection for these industries,
the Congress sometimes plays a major role in determining
the manner in which existing trade laws are implemented
with respect to a particular sector. Similarly the president
plays a major role in shaping the nature of the broad trade
policy framework enacted by the Congress. The chief executive usually proposes major new trade legislation, and
veto and other powers enable him to exert considerable
influence over the nature of this legislation as it works its
way through the Congress. As Pastor (1980) emphasizes,
one must analyze the interactive process between the president and the Congress to understand the formulation and
execution of modern foreign economic policy.

   Policymaking by three key government groups is
studied: the Congress, the ITC, and the president and his
advisers.[5] After the presentation in this chapter of the general analytical framework to be followed, separate chapters
are devoted to each of these decision-making centers. A
brief survey of trade policymaking powers of the three
government units is given in each of the chapters, followed
by a more detailed discussion of their possible behavior
patterns and an analysis of actual decision making on particular import issues. In the chapter on the Congress, this
latter analysis focuses on the formulation and implementation of the Trade Act of 1974. Among other issues examined is the manner in which the Congress radically
changed the initial bill proposed by the president and then

utilized certain provisions of the act to secure trade concessions for particular industries. A statistical analysis of various political and economic factors that influenced the voting pattern of members of Congress on the bill is also included.

The issues studied in the ITC chapter include the appointment process to the commission and the set of political and economic factors that best explain the commission's decisions in import relief cases. The chapter on policymaking at the presidential level statistically analyzes the factors influencing whether the president accepts affirmative ITC findings in these cases, as well as the private sector and congressional pressures applied on the president just prior to the implementation of the trigger price mechanism for the steel industry. Furthermore various hypotheses designed to explain interindustry variations in the tariff cuts made in general tariff-reducing negotiations are tested by regression analysis utilizing data on the actual cuts offered by the United States during the Tokyo Round of multilateral trade negotiations. The study ends with a chapter that summarizes the main conclusions and suggests certain institutional changes aimed at improving the formulation and implementation of trade policies.

This study makes no attempt to deal with all the different forms of import policies nor does it explore the full range of interrelationships within the government or between the government and various private groups. Instead it focuses on a limited number of U.S. import policies for the purpose of trying to discover the types of economic and political factors that shape these policies. By selecting several kinds of policies over which different parts of the government have policymaking authority, it is hoped that some useful generalizations can be made.

1.2 The Positive Theory of Trade Policy Determination

In trying to explain actual behavior, it is sometimes helpful first to specify conditions under which the observed behavior is not likely to occur and then to modify these assumptions in order to make the framework conform more closely with reality. By considering the behavioral effects of lifting the various restrictive assumptions, the investigator can often gain a better appreciation of the key factors that account for the particular behavior than by trying directly to understand the interrelationships among a host of complex real-world conditions. This simplifying approach will be followed in presenting the positive theory of trade policy determination.

Suppose the following conditions hold: (1) voters directly determine by majority vote whether a particular public policy is put into effect; (2) only one policy issue is to be decided within voters' time horizons; (3) there is perfect information as well as the absence of any costs of voting or of redistributing income among individuals; (4) there are fixed supplies of labor and capital that are freely mobile among industries within the economy; (5) the preferences of all individuals for goods and services are identical;[6] (6) perfect competition prevails; and (7) all goods are produced under constant returns to scale technology. The objective of each individual is to maximize his real income, which depends only on the goods and services he consumes.

The policy issue to be decided is whether to introduce a particular set of import duties or to adopt a free trade policy. Assume, as trade economists often do, that the country under consideration is small in the sense that the international prices of the goods it trades are not affected by the volume of its imports or exports and that there are no domestic economic distortions or inefficiencies. Given all of these assumptions, it follows on the basis of standard trade theory that the productive factor used relatively intensively in the production of export goods gains under free trade as compared with import protection, whereas the factor used relatively intensively in import-competing production loses under free trade compared to the tariff situation. Thus if the nature of technology is such that a higher ratio of capital to labor is required in producing export goods than in producing import-competing goods (that is, capital is used relatively intensively in the production of export goods), capitalists will prefer free trade to the market outcome under import duties, since their real income will be higher under free trade. By contrast, labor is better off under the tariff situation and therefore will favor this policy. Should import-competing goods be capital intensive compared with export goods, the policy preferences of capitalists and workers would be reversed.

A further important result from trade theory, given the previous assumptions, is that the individuals who gain under free trade are capable of fully compensating the losers for the real income loss they incur under free trade compared to the tariff situation. Moreover, the gainers will still be better off after undertaking this compensating income redistribution than they would be under the tariff situation; however, the individuals who would gain if import duties are introduced are unable to compensate those who lose with the tariff without the gainers ending up worse off than they would be under free trade. Because of these differences, economists say that free trade is potentially superior to import protection (given the various assumptions made), since it is possible to make some people better off under free trade compared to a tariff situation without making anyone worse off. (It also follows that it is possible to make everyone better off under free trade.)[7]

Under the voting framework assumed up to this point, these results mean that free trade will always be selected over a policy of tariffs. If the productive factors who gain under free trade represent a majority of voters, it is not necessary for them to compensate the losers under free trade in order to achieve the policy they favor. But if capitalists are the gainers under free trade and they are in the minority, they will have to tie a particular income redistribution scheme to the free trade vote that will overcompensate enough losers to secure a majority vote for the free trade policy.[8]

When various assumptions made at the outset of this analysis are modified to make the framework correspond more closely with real-world conditions, the conclusion that a policy of free trade will always be selected by voters over protectionism no longer holds, even though free trade is potentially superior in national real-income terms to a system of import duties. Suppose, for example, an individual must incur certain costs in order to vote. The so-called free rider problem arises under these circumstances and may lead to the selection of the welfare-inferior policy. This problem arises because trade policy has the characteristic of a public good in that a beneficiary from a particular trade policy such as free trade cannot be excluded from the benefits, even though he does not contribute to the costs of obtaining the policy.[9]

To be more specific, suppose that workers are the gainers under free trade but that they must incur certain voting costs (which are, however, assumed to be less than their income gains) for this policy to be implemented.[10] If an individual worker votes for free trade and this policy option is selected by a majority of voters, he gains as compared with the tariff situation. If, however, he does not vote and free trade is selected, he gains even more since he still enjoys the benefits but does not pay the voting costs. Thus there is an incentive for each worker not to act on his true preferences, particularly when his net gains under free trade are relatively small, in the hopes of free riding on the voting of other workers, who are sufficiently numerous to secure the required majority vote. Because of this reasoning, only a comparatively small number of workers may in fact vote.

By contrast, suppose that the number of capitalists is relatively small so that although their aggregate gain under the tariff is less than the aggregate gain to workers under free trade, their per capita gain is substantially above their per capita costs of voting. As Olson (1965) points out, the capitalists will be more likely to vote (for tariffs) than the workers since their individual stake in the outcome is greater than for the individual worker. Consequently the tariff option may receive a larger number of votes than free trade, even though the latter policy yields a potentially higher real national income.

Probably the most important reason for divergences between what is economically most efficient and what actually occurs in the political marketplace is the lack of perfect information and the fact that acquiring and disseminating information is costly.[11] Suppose, for example, that in the situation described only a certain proportion of the workers and capitalists know whether they gain or lose under free trade versus protection. Also suppose that it pays the workers who know they gain under free trade to incur the costs of informing their fellow workers of their true economic interests, thereby securing the adoption of the free trade option. (Again assume that there are no costs of voting.) But since the funds needed for the informational effort can be raised only by voluntary contributions, the free rider problem arises. Each worker in the knowledgeable group has an incentive not to contribute in the expectation that others will contribute enough to obtain the adoption of free trade. If there are a large number of individuals in this group and their net gain is relatively small, few may contribute to the efforts to disseminate information. If, however, the net per capita gain to all or some of the capitalists possessing the knowledge needed to know their economic interests is relatively large, either because their numbers are small or some own a large share of the capital stock, there is a greater likelihood that the funds needed to inform other capitalists of their interests will be obtained through voluntary contributions. Consequently, as in the voting cost illustration, the tariff policy may be selected over free trade.

Recognizing that most public policies are decided by elected representatives of the voters rather than directly by the voters is another step that brings the tariff determination framework closer to reality. By itself, however, representative voting will not change the conclusions derived under the initial set of simplifying assumptions. Elected representatives will merely be intermediaries carrying out the wishes of the majority of their electorates. If they fail to do so, they will be replaced through the competitive political process whereby representatives are chosen by voters. However, if the existence of voting costs and imperfect knowledge are taken into account, as well as the fact that elected representatives make decisions on many issues besides trade policy, the likelihood increases that the most economically efficient trade policy may not be chosen.

Due to imperfect knowledge, elected officials may not be fully aware of the economic interests of their constituents, and their constituents may not be familiar with all the policy stances they have taken that affect their interests. Consequently a particular group of voters may have to engage in time-consuming and costly lobbying activities to bring its viewpoint to the attention of legislators. Similarly office-seekers need funds for running their election campaigns in order to inform the voters of how they have served them or will do so in the future.[12] These conditions mean that it may be to an industry's advantage to organize for the purpose of raising funds through voluntary contributions and then to use these funds to lobby for import protection by disseminating information favorable to their case and by providing campaign contributions to office-seekers who support their position. If an industry is able to secure sufficient funds from its members, it will select the level of lobbying expenditures that yields the degree of protection that maximizes the difference between the benefits from protection and the costs of lobbying.

Two models developed within this public choice framework to explain the differences among industries in their ability to obtain import protection or resist cuts in protection are the so-called common interest or pressure group model and the adding machine model. The first, and best-known, of these models has been developed by such writers as Olson (1965), Stigler (1974), Pincus (1975), Brock and Magee (1978), and Findlay and Wellisz (1982). This common interest or pressure group model assumes that capitalists in import-competing industries favor import protection for their industries because the resulting higher domestic prices bring them income gains in the short run when capital is relatively immobile among industries.[13] However, while all import-competing industries would like the government to restrict imports in their industries, they differ in their ability to overcome the free rider problem associated with efforts to raise lobbying funds through voluntary contributions. According to Olson (1965), the formation of an industry organization that is able to obtain sufficient funds from its members to lobby effectively is more likely if the number of firms in the industry is small and benefits from protection are unevenly distributed among the firms, since under these conditions the benefits to each firm, or at least some firms, increase.[14] Pincus (1975) adds that the costs of coordinating and monitoring a pressure group tend to reduce effective lobbying activity if an industry is widely dispersed. These points suggest the hypothesis that the level of protection in an industry should be higher and the ability of the industry to resist across-the-board tariff-cutting efforts should be greater, the fewer the number of firms in the sector and the higher both the seller concentration and geographic concentration ratios.[15]

Olson (1983) has recently argued that even those economic groups that can be organized into effective voluntary associations will usually not do so until some time after their common interests emerge. Exceptional opportunities for economic gain or economic shocks that seriously threaten existing income and employment levels may be needed for such groups to organize. Thus, on the basis of this reasoning, one would expect levels of industry protection or changes in these levels to be negatively related to industry growth rates in output and employment and positively associated with import penetration ratios or changes in these ratios. Furthermore the voting behavior of members of Congress on trade policy issues should reflect the concerns of industries faced with high and rising import penetration levels. For example, the higher the proportion of voters in a district who are employed in industries facing significant import competition, the more likely that the member of Congress representing this district will vote in a protectionist manner.

The adding machine model formulated by Caves (1976) also stresses the existence of imperfect knowledge among voters, as well as the fact that voting decisions are made on the basis of a candidate's views on a multitude of public policy issues. An elected official cannot possibly satisfy every voter on every issue. Therefore in order to maximize the probability of his or her reelection, the position he or she adopts on any issue is one that represents the views of the majority of those voters who are most concerned about the issue. As far as import policy is concerned, this means those individuals employed in industries subject to competition. Furthermore in influencing levels of protection (or cuts in these levels) for different import-competing industries, an elected official tends to favor industries with the largest number of voters. Consequently on the basis of this model, one expects a positive relationship between levels of protection or changes in protective levels and the number of employees in an industry. Caves also argues that protection will tend to be high and duty cuts low in industries in which value added per worker is low (or the labor intensity of production is high).

Caves further believes that elected officials are more responsive to an industry composed of a large number of small firms than one that is highly concentrated. This hypothesis is opposite to the one formulated by the adherents to the common interest group model.[16] Both the adding machine and the common interest group models will be empirically tested in chapter 4, using the depth of the Tokyo Round duty cuts across industries and the levels of industry tariffs.

1.3 Autonomous Behavior by Public Officials

Another important implication of recognizing that political markets are imperfect is that elected officials may not simply be intermediaries whose behavior reflects the wishes of the electorate or some part of it. Instead they may pursue their own public policy goals on many occasions and still retain their elected positions. This point has been stressed by such political scientists as Nordlinger (1981) and Krasner (1978) and also comes out clearly in various studies by political scientists of the behavior of members of Congress (Fenno 1978), and of the president (Neustadt 1976), and it is implicitly accepted in some of the models outlined in the next section where social values are introduced into the preference framework.[17]

Autonomous behavior on the part of public officials is most likely to occur either when voters are not significantly affected economically by alternative policies or the support for different policy actions is roughly balanced among groups that matter to elected officials. For example, the vote of a member of Congress on free trade versus protection may be of little concern to voters in many congressional districts and will not affect the individual's reelection prospects to any appreciable extent. In this case an elected official can follow his or her own preferences or, if the person has none, simply follow the party's position on the issue. The name recognition advantage of incumbency, coupled with the financial and institutional entry barriers faced by potential competitors for national office, gives established legislators a certain degree of freedom to follow their own preferences rather than vote the legislative goals of common interest groups that provide campaign funds needed to acquaint voters with candidates and their programs. More generally the ability of public officials to disseminate information themselves and to alter the distribution of both the benefits provided and the costs imposed by the state enables officials on some occasions to act on their own public policy preferences, even though these preferences diverge, at least initially, from those held by most voters. In other words the state itself can be highly effective in lobbying for a particular policy and use its own power in ways to offset opposition from private groups.[18]

The extent to which public officials can act autonomously depends on the particular part of the government's institutional structure in which they serve. With respect to the key government actors in trade policy matters—the president, the Congress, and the ITC—one would expect the president to have the greatest ability to follow his own public policy preferences since his position provides unparalleled opportunities to communicate his views to voters and to diffuse political opposition. Furthermore the number of import-competing industries vitally concerned about trade policy because of their international competitive position is likely to represent only a very small proportion of his electorate. The president's special responsibilities in the foreign policy area also serve to diminish the weight he attaches to the views of import-injured sectors and tend to make him more liberal in his trade policy position than Congress as a whole. Nevertheless if a presidential or congressional election is imminent and the president's political party faces a close contest, the president may feel that it is necessary to implement the wishes of such industries to help ensure his own reelection or that of congressional members of his party.

The ability of individual members of Congress to pursue their own interests may be either less or greater than that of the president. It is quite possible, for example, for a significant proportion of the jobs in the electoral district of a member of the House of Representatives to be tied directly or indirectly to an industry being seriously injured by import competition. In these circumstances representatives risk almost certain defeat if they do not actively support import protection or some alternative form of assistance for the industry. In contrast in some districts trade policy may be generally perceived as having an insignificant effect on economic welfare. Consequently persons representing such districts can pursue either their free trade or protectionist preferences without affecting their reelection chances. If they have no particular preference for either policy, they might also use their influence for such purposes as trying to secure the support of other legislators for a policy in which they are interested,

strengthening their position with the congressional leadership, or asserting the power of the Congress in its relations
with the president.

Since senators generally represent more populous and
industrially diversified political units than House members, it is less likely that the proportion of workers employed in import-injured industries will be so high that a
senator is forced to adopt a protectionist posture in order
to remain in office. (States like Michigan, where the auto
and auto parts industry dominates manufacturing activity,
are obvious exceptions.) Because of their more diversified
constituencies, senators are also more likely to try to build
political support by promoting collective goals of wide appeal, such as reducing wasteful government expenditures,
rather than by catering to narrow interest groups. Furthermore, compared to congressmen, they are better able to
project the image of successfully promoting these more
universal goals, as well as to diffuse pressures from particular interest groups. These structural considerations, together with the special responsibilities of the Senate in
foreign policy matters, suggest that one might expect the
Senate to be less protectionist than the House.

The manner in which the two legislative bodies are organized has the effect of reversing this conclusion, however.
Compared to the Senate, the House is a much more struc-
tured body in which freedom of expression of the individual member is subordinated to the will of the group.[19]
Trade bills typically reach the floor of the House with a
closed rule that either prohibits amendments or permits
consideration of only a limited number. Since the committee that considers most trade bills, the Ways and Means
Committee, has a strong tradition of behaving in a manner
that House members will regard as responsible, it is also
difficult to include protectionist provisions for particular
industries in bills that come before the House as a whole.[20]

The Senate is a more individualistic institution in which committee chairpersons possess less authority and in which unlimited debate and an unlimited number of amendments are typically permitted after trade bills are sent from the Finance Committee to the Senate as a whole. Because of these organizational differences, some argue that the Senate is more responsive to the demands of various interest groups and therefore tends to be more protectionist than the House.[21] Thus, on balance, it would seem that senators have a greater ability to provide import protection to particular sectors, even though the incentive to do so may be greater among congressmen. One outcome of this situation may be that protection legislation in the House is more likely to take the form of general, nonindustry-specific provisions, whereas in the Senate it manifests itself to a greater extent as import relief for particular industries.

Other key groups of government officials who can affect the nature of trade policy are presidential appointees (with the consent of the Senate) to the ITC and nonelected trade officials employed in the various departments making up the executive branch. Congress has deliberately tried to minimize the possibility that members of the ITC will be influenced either by private interest groups or the president and Congress by not allowing reappointment after their nine-year term and by prescribing in some detail the way they are to implement the trade laws Congress passes. Consequently one would expect that these officials would not be much influenced by current economic and political pressures. In seeking personal satisfaction through respect by others for his decisions, each commissioner is likely to try to follow closely the economic guidelines established by Congress. Due to the general nature of these guidelines, however, there is considerable room for differences among the commissioners on how best to implement the criteria set forth in the law. These differences in interpretation will depend mainly on the differences among the commissioners in their background knowledge and experience prior to joining the ITC. This background will, of course, be taken into consideration in the appointment process.

Political appointees and high-level civil servants in the main departments of the executive branch are constrained by the preferences of the president, but they play an important advisory role in shaping the specifics of trade policies and sometimes the general nature of these policies as well. Since there are significant divergences in views concerning appropriate trade policies among such agencies as the Departments of State, Commerce, Treasury, Labor, and Agriculture, an understanding of the manner in which trade decisions are reached in the executive branch and the relative influence of these different agencies and their leaders at the White House level is also important for understanding how trade policies are determined.

1.4 Modifying the Positive Theory of Trade Policy Determination: Social and Interpersonal Effects

The public choice theory outlined in section 1.2 was based on the assumptions that all individuals in the economy seek to maximize their welfare and that individual welfare depends only on the goods and services a person consumes directly. It is evident, however, that such considerations as equity, social justice, and patriotism may also affect public policy choices. Thus the fact that a high proportion of the labor force employed in textiles consists of low-income workers may account partly for the protection granted this industry in many developed countries. The desire to protect the incomes of underprivileged groups, whether defined by income level, sex, race, or regional location, such as depressed regions, can, in other words, be important to the study of protectionism, though it does not itself explain the choice of import barriers rather than the use of other policies to redistribute income to the concerned group.

If a concern for other citizens helps to explain protection, then what prompts such altruistic attitudes? Arrow gives three reasons why an individual undertakes actions that are or seem to be expressions of altruism.[22] First, the welfare of the individual may depend not only on the goods he consumes but also on the economic welfare of others. An altruistic relationship exists if the individual's welfare decreases when the welfare of others decreases.[23] Interpersonal relationships of this type are excluded from the public choice theory previously described. Second, the individual may not only derive satisfaction from seeing someone else's satisfaction increased but may also gain satisfaction from the fact that he has contributed to that satisfaction. Third, an individual may be motivated entirely by his own egotistic satisfaction, but "there is an implicit social contract that each performs duties for others in a way calculated to enhance the satisfaction of all": an argument that implies enlightened self-interest.[24]

Of these reasons for altruistic behavior, the last may have particular relevance to protectionist policies. Individuals may support a tariff increase outside their own industry because they think this action enhances their chances of receiving tariff protection should their industry come under severe import competition in the future. Or they may believe this support improves their chances of obtaining some other form of public assistance that they may desire in the future. This idea serves as the basis for regarding tariffs as a type of insurance policy.[25] Workers and capital owners who are risk averse wish to avoid human and physical capital losses due to sudden and significant increases in imports that compete with the domestic products they produce. However, private markets to insure against this risk do not exist, apparently for reasons of inadequate data or "moral hazard." The import relief legislation involving recommendations from the ITC can, for example, be viewed as a means of providing the desired insurance. If this view is adopted, it still does not explain why the implicit contractual behavior agreed on by voters to provide relief against injurious import competition takes the form of import restriction, since there are other policies, such as income or production subsidies, that would aid the injured producers to the same extent but lessen the real income burden on the rest of the economy.

A final reason for altruistic behavior noted by Phelps (1975) deserves mention. There should, he states, "be room too in the taxonomy for acts of altruism in which there is 'nothing personal,' only a generalized regard for human rights, social codes, business 'ethics,' and so on."[26] As Phelps says, it is best thought of as a moralistic constraint on utility maximization rather than as part of one's utility function. Protection may also reflect goals other than equity, enlightened self-interest, or simple altruism. In his seminal analysis of the scientific tariff, Johnson (1960) explored the nature of the optimal tariff structure to promote collective goals such as industrialization, self-sufficiency, a way of life, and military preparedness.

Several writers have emphasized the importance of social values and interpersonal effects as the basis for trade policy determination. Their analyses can be grouped into three general models: (1) the status quo model, (2) the social change model, and (3) the foreign policy model.

The status quo model was named by Lavergne (1983), who hypothesized that current duty levels and recent duty changes will be positively correlated with historical duty levels. Government officials have a conservative respect for the status quo, he argues, based either on a regard for existing property rights (even in the form of rents generated by protection) or on a cautious response to the uncertainty associated with the effects of change. Still another reason he suggests in support of his hypothesis is that government officials wish to avoid large adjustment costs.

Corden (1974) set forth the key idea in the status quo model when he introduced the notion of the conservative social welfare function. He states that this social welfare function is based on the income distribution target that "any significant absolute reductions in real incomes of any significant section of the community should be avoided. This is not quite the same as setting up the existing distribution as the best, but comes close to it, and so can indeed be described as 'conservative.'"[27]

Cheh (1974) also used the status quo notion in hypothesizing that governments aim at minimizing short-run labor adjustment costs (thus minimizing significant absolute reductions in income) in determining the pattern of duty cuts across industries in a tariff-reducing multilateral trade negotiation. Variables used to measure the ability of workers in an industry to adjust to duty cuts or increased import competition include the percentage of unskilled workers, the percentage of workers over forty-five years of age, the proportion of workers in rural areas, the height of the initial duty, and the growth rate of an industry's output. In testing his model, Cheh hypothesizes that there should be a positive relationship between the first three variables and changes in industry tariff levels negotiated in the Kennedy Round on the grounds that unskilled, older workers living in rural areas take longer than other workers to find new jobs. He also expects low tariff cuts in high-duty industries since a given percentage cut in a high-duty item tends to reduce its import price relatively more (and thus put more adjustment pressure on domestic producers) than the same percentage cut in a low-duty item. On the other hand, since rapid industry growth facilitates adjustment to duty reductions, he posits that growth rates and the extent of duty cuts will be positively correlated. While Cheh confines the test of his model to the duty-cutting decisions of the president during a multilateral trade negotiation, one can also try to ascertain whether the legislative actions of Congress in the trade area or the import injury decisions of the ITC are consistent with the adjustment assistance hypothesis.

In the status quo model the basic objective of government officials is to prevent any significant reduction in the real income level of any significant income group in the economy. According to some writers, however, in setting the pattern of duty cuts, government officials often seek to promote social goals that involve significant changes in the pattern of income distribution or in other social interrelationships. This social change model is illustrated by the analyses of Ball (1967), Constantopoulos (1974), and Fieleke (1976). These writers maintain that U.S. government officials seek on social justice grounds to reduce the degree of income inequality in the economy by raising the living standards of the lowest income groups. Consequently in trade negotiations they shield low-income, unskilled workers from the job-displacing and (nominal) wage-reducing effects of tariff reductions. They hypothesize therefore that tariffs and other trade barriers will be high (and cuts in protection low) in industries intensively using low-income, unskilled labor. Industry measures of these characteristics are average wages, value added per worker, and the proportion of unskilled workers.

The support of elected officials and the general public for fair trade legislation illustrates another type of change sought on social grounds. Protection against import increases resulting from subsidies by foreign governments, dumping by foreign firms, or pricing policies by communist countries that are unrelated to actual costs is easier to obtain than protection from import increases resulting from open, free-market competition because the first type of import pressure is considered socially undesirable by many. One would expect, therefore, that industries seeking protection would often emphasize the "unfair" nature of foreign competition. Import policies aimed at promoting a collective good, such as national defense, as well as a particular way of life associated with an economic sector or at controlling economic externalities that affect the environment, also fit into the social change model.

Because of the free rider problem, one would generally not expect voters who are motivated by equity and other social concerns to be organized into politically effective pressure groups. Kau and Rubin (1982) find, however, that in some fields, among them environmental matters, public interest groups have influenced congressional voting even though the members of the groups do not benefit as producers from the legislation they seek. They believe that membership in public interest groups is determined by ideological factors and suggest that members are best viewed as purchasing a good they term "participation."

The last of the three models that emphasize the importance of social values for understanding import policies in contrast to short-run economic self-interest is the foreign policy model. In this model government officials identify with the nation as a social unit engaged in economic, political, and security relations with other national units. Helleiner (1977) suggests that government officials in trade negotiations adopt a mercantilistic attitude in their bargaining with other countries and try to obtain the greatest cuts in protection from others in return for the least cuts by their own country.[28] One obvious consideration affecting a country's ability to obtain cuts in foreign protection on products of export interest is the country's willingness to reduce its own trade barriers. Since the less-developed countries have generally been unwilling to match the cuts offered by the industrial countries, Helleiner hypothesizes that duty levels in industrial countries will be higher (and duty cuts less) on products of export interest to the developing countries than on items supplied by countries practicing reciprocity. He utilizes the level of wages across industries as well as an economies-of-scale variable to indicate those manufactured products in which the developing countries have an export interest.

Lavergne (1983) also predicts on the basis of Helleiner's analysis that U.S. tariff levels will be high (and duty cuts low) in product lines in which the Japanese are important exporters to the United States, due to the reluctance of Japan to open up its domestic markets. In contrast he expects the opposite relationship for U.S.–Canadian trade because of the economic and political importance of Canada to the United States.

Still another relationship suggested by Helleiner's bargaining framework is that a country will be more willing to grant trade concessions to another country the more extensive is its direct foreign investment in this other country. The bargaining strength of the foreign country is enhanced by its ability to restrict the flow of earnings back to the investing country.

Import policy is also used for foreign policy purposes other than mercantilistic economic gains. For example, reductions in protection on products of special export interest to particular countries are sometimes made by government officials to promote the international political or security goals of the United States. Concern over the international distribution of income also is sometimes a motivating factor in shaping import policies.

The three models described that emphasize the importance of social concerns as a behavior force—the status quo, the social change, and the foreign policy models—along with the two models in section 1.2 that stress short-run self-interest behavior—the pressure group and adding machine models—will be evaluated empirically in chapter 4 by relating Tokyo Round duty cuts and duty levels across industries to industry characteristics that serve as proxies for behavior patterns on which the different models are based.

In general one would expect that the social and interpersonal effects underlying the three models described in this section would motivate the president's trade policy behavior more than the behavior of Congress. Individual members of Congress may be as concerned personally about the economic welfare of socially deserving but politically unorganized groups or about protecting the general environment as the president, but their greater vulnerability to self-interest-oriented pressure groups and their more limited freedom to behave autonomously restrict their ability to act on these concerns. These are the same reasons why Congress is likely to be less liberal on trade policy matters than the president.

The introduction of social and interpersonal concerns into a public choice framework not only helps to explain why certain politically weak sectors receive import protection but to account for why legislation is passed that involves significant cuts in U.S. tariffs. Whether it is for ethical or long-run self-interest reasons or because of interpersonal utility effects, most voters and elected officials are concerned about their country's long-run economic relations with other nations. The U.S. electorate seems to accept the view that promoting economic prosperity in other countries is not only a desirable goal in itself but contributes to domestic prosperity through increased U.S. exports and reduces the chances of U.S. involvement in international political and military conflicts. Therefore they are prepared to support such economic policies as reciprocal duty reductions and even zero-duty treatment for the exports of developing countries, provided they are assured that such actions will not jeopardize their own economic interests or those of other domestic groups for which they have altruistic concerns.

Because of their special national responsibilities, top government officials in the executive branch and Congress tend to identify with the state as a political-economic unit and find it politically advantageous to promote international economic policies that are perceived to contribute to U.S. economic prosperity and international political stability. A president can usually rely on general public support when he requests legislative authority for a reciprocal duty-reducing multilateral negotiation that he promises will promote these national goals without injuring any domestic sector. Thus some import-competing industries that are already facing intense foreign competition have found on the basis of past experience that they can best promote their interests by trying to secure an exception to the general duty-cutting rule for their industries rather than by opposing the entire duty-cutting negotiation.

1.5 Shifting Economic Structures and Protectionism

In the preceding sections, various hypotheses have been outlined concerning the political-economic characteristics of industries that influence how successful they are in obtaining import protection from the government. According to the common interest group model, the number of firms and the degree of seller and geographic concentration in an industry are the key factors determining an industry's ability to secure protection. In contrast, one form of the status quo model points to the ease with which an industry's workers can adjust to job-displacing economic changes as the most important characteristic affecting an industry's chances of receiving import protection.

Implicit in these and the other models is the assumption that import protection is perceived to be desirable policy for the industry, either by those employed in the industry or government officials and other citizens; however, if, for example, imports in an industry are negligible and exports are high, such an assumption is not likely to be warranted. Clearly the structure of the economy and the manner in which it is changing affect people's perception of the need to protect different industries. The intensity of these views in turn affects the interindustry levels of protection that are likely to emerge out of the political process.

In undertaking statistical tests of the explanatory significance of the various political-economic characteristics emphasized in the different models, it is therefore necessary to include variables that reflect the manner in which an industry's competitive condition affects the degree of protection it is likely to receive. For example, in trying to explain changes in interindustry protection, revealed comparative advantage measures such as an industry's ratio of exports to imports and the ratio of imports to consumption are often introduced to control for these effects.

Scholars interested in explaining changes in level of protection over time have also stressed the importance of shifts in basic comparative cost conditions. For example, the hegemonic model of regime change, associated with such writers as Kindleberger (1973), Krasner (1976), and Keohane (1984), relates worldwide shifts in trade policy to the extent to which a single nation dominates world trade. The reasoning behind the model is as follows. An open international trading system has elements of a public good in the sense that if one country reduces its trade barriers under the most-favored-nation principle, other countries benefit from the improved export opportunities this creates for them, even if they do not make reciprocal cuts themselves. Consequently there is an incentive for any individual country to free ride, hoping that others will reduce their trade barriers. The net result may be the failure to secure a balanced multilateral set of significant trade barrier cuts even though they would benefit all participants. Using the same type of argument put forth in discussing the common interest group model, this outcome is less likely if one country has such a strong comparative cost position that it dominates world trade. The dominant nation is so large in trading terms that the costs to it of free rides by other countries tend to be small compared to its gains. Furthermore the large country may be able to use its power to force smaller members to practice reciprocity.[29]

Proponents of the hegemonic model point to the dominant trade position of Great Britain during a large part of the nineteenth century and of the United States in the immediate post–World War II period to account for the creation of liberal trading policies throughout much of the world in these periods. The decline in U.S. hegemony since the 1960s and 1970s because of the increased international competitiveness of the European Community and Japan is also advanced as the explanation for increased protectionism in recent years.[30]

Krauss (1978), Nowzad (1978), and Cassing, McKeown, and Ochs (1984) have hypothesized that national economic conditions also affect levels of protection over the business cycle. Low growth rates and high unemployment increase the likelihood of a general shift to protectionist policies, whereas prosperous conditions improve the chances that liberal trade policies will be adopted. A test of this hypothesis by Takacs (1981), using the number of import injury cases coming before the ITC as the dependent variable, supported the hypothesis as far as the number of petitions filed was concerned but not in terms of the actual number of affirmative decisions.

Although efforts to explain shifts over time between liberal and protectionist trade policies are worthwhile, this subject will not receive much attention in this study.[31] Instead the study is mainly concerned with the differences at any one time in the nature of responses by the Congress, the ITC, and the president to requests for protection and with the differential ability of industries characterized by different political-economic features to obtain protection from the government.

Other aspects of import policy that will not be considered here are premium-seeking (a term coined by Bhagwati 1982) and revenue-seeking activities. The first term refers to the situation Krueger (1974) analyzed in which the imposition of quantitative restrictions leads to competition among individuals for the premium-fetching import licenses associated with quotas. Bhagwati and Srinivasan (1980) have also suggested that economic agents will compete for a slice of the tariff revenues resulting from the adoption of a protective tariff and term this activity revenue-seeking. In contrast to these activities, however, this study will focus on what the latter two authors describe as tariff seeking: the efforts by various economic groups to increase import duties or resist duty cuts.

1.6 Summary

This chapter has presented the public choice framework that will be used in analyzing U.S. import policy and set forth the main hypotheses about trade policy behavior that will be considered in more detail in later chapters. If political markets were perfect in much the same sense that economists mean when describing perfect economic competition, governments would not adopt national welfare-reducing policies such as restrictive import policies. However, the existence of such real world conditions as imperfect information, costs of redistributing income or taking political action, and income distribution concerns by public officials give rise to the possibility that the most economically efficient trade policies will not be adopted.

Just what the key political-economic factors are that account for differences among import-competing sectors in their ability to obtain government protection from imports is a matter of considerable disagreement among writers on the subject. Five different models attempting to explain interindustry differences in both levels of protection and changes in protection have been described in the chapter. The key political-economic characteristic of an industry that each emphasizes as the main determinant of the industry's ability to obtain protection or resist liberalization can be summarized as follows:

• Common interest or pressure group model: The ability of an industry to organize for the purpose of raising funds for lobbying activities.

• Adding machine model: The voting strength of an industry.

• Status quo model: The historical levels of an industry's protection and the ability of the industry to adjust to increased import competition due either to proposed decreases in protection or to changes in basic economic conditions.

• Social change model: The income and skill levels of workers in the industry, the nature of the international competition faced by the industry, and its importance in terms of promoting such social changes as an improved national defense capability and better environmental conditions.

• Foreign policy model: The bargaining ability, political importance, and income levels of the countries from which competing imports are supplied.

Both the common interest group and adding machine models are based on a view of the political decision-making process that considers the state largely as an intermediary responding to the short-run economic interests of various pressure groups. In contrast the other three models rest on a view of the political process that considers private citizens and government officials as either taking a long-run view of their self-interest or being concerned about the economic welfare of other groups and the state.

The pattern of interindustry protection is influenced not only by differences among industries in their ability to succeed in the political marketplace but in their ability to compete in economic markets since the latter factor affects the perceived need for protection. This means that industry measures of comparative cost conditions and general economic vitality must be included in analyses of protection across industries.

Economic competitiveness and general macroeconomic conditions also play an important role in explanations of U.S. shifts between liberal and protective trade policies over time. The hegemonic model of regime trade and the cyclical theory of trade policy determination illustrate these points. This study, however, will focus mainly on differences in protectionist behavior among industries and units of government rather than over time.

Two other important and interrelated themes of the chapter are that government officials behave autonomously on many occasions and that the nature of trade policy actions depends on the particular part of the government involved in the decision-making process. Some of the main hypotheses set forth concerning the president, the Congress, and the ITC are as follows:

• The president tends to pursue more liberal trade policies than Congress.

• The nature of the president's trade policies is affected by the structure of decision making in the executive branch and the relative influence at the White House level of the various agencies involved in trade matters.

• The ITC is less likely to be influenced by protectionist pressures than either Congress or the president.

• Due to differences in the way the two bodies of Congress are organized, the Senate is more receptive to requests for protection from particular industries than the House.

• The interaction between the president and the Congress on trade issues plays a major role in shaping policies.

• Both the president and the Congress are more likely to adopt protectionist measures just prior to an election.

Since trade policy is largely carried out by the Congress, the ITC, and the president, the format of the study will be to analyze import policy decision making by each of these three units of the federal government. The final chapter summarizes the main conclusions and makes some suggestions for improving the policymaking process in the trade field.

2   Import Policy at the Congressional Level

The Constitution grants Congress the power "to regulate commerce with foreign nations" and to levy duties as well as other forms of taxes.[1] The president also possesses constitutional powers relating to international trade because of his responsibility for conducting foreign relations (Article 2, section 2 of the Constitution). However, the courts have held the authority of Congress to be preeminent whenever presidential actions have conflicted with acts of Congress.[2] Consequently it is appropriate to begin an analysis of U.S. import policy by examining the ways in which Congress responds to pressures for both protectionism and import liberalization.

The first section of this chapter outlines the means that Congress uses to shape import policy and discusses its efforts to achieve the desired balance of delegating the details of policy implementation to the President while still determining the basic nature of U.S. import policy. The following section then utilizes the analytical framework presented in chapter 1 to consider in more detail how members of Congress are likely to react to trade policy pressures from various sources. In the final section, hypotheses developed in the preceding section and in chapter 1 are tested or illustrated by examining congressional behavior during the formulation and implementation of the Trade Act of 1974.

2.1 Congressional Controls over Import Policy

The main means by which Congress regulates foreign trade is through legislation. An outstanding feature of trade legislation in this century is the extensive delegation of powers to the president that has accompanied the import policies Congress has enacted.[3] Since the Tariff Act of 1897, the president has had the power to impose countervailing duties against foreign goods that are subsidized upon exportation.[4] In the 1920s Congress also provided the president with the authority to levy antidumping duties, to impose duties on or even to exclude foreign goods in retaliation against both unfair practices in import trade and unreasonable or discriminatory import policies on the part of other countries, and to modify tariff rates to a limited degree in order to equalize differences in production costs.[5] The most notable grant of power occurred in 1934, when Congress authorized the president to negotiate trade agreements with other countries and granted him the power to reduce duties by as much as 50 percent in return for reciprocal reductions by other nations.[6] This action was significant not only because of the magnitude of the tariff-changing powers given the chief executive but because it marked an end to detailed tariff setting by Congress on a regular and comprehensive basis. Since the Trade Agreements Act of 1934, Congress has periodically extended the authority of the president to reduce tariffs on a reciprocal basis and has provided him with additional duty-cutting authority.

Much of the history of U.S. trade policy after 1934 may be interpreted as a continuing effort by Congress to work out an acceptable arrangement with the executive branch that avoids the frustrations and political risks of detailed policymaking in the trade area and yet ensures that congressional intentions are closely followed in policy implementation.[7] Between 1934 and 1962 the major way in which Congress exercised control over the president's tariff-reducing actions was to extend his authority to enter into trade agreements with other countries only for short periods—usually three years. This provided Congress the opportunity periodically to stop further duty reductions.

Frequently Congress used the renewal occasions to restrict the duty-reducing authority of the president. The escape clause and peril point provisions included in the extensions of the trade agreements program in the 1940s and 1950s illustrate this method of control. The escape clause established an investigatory procedure for determining whether increased imports resulting from a previously granted tariff concession were causing or threatening serious injury to the domestic industry that was producing directly competitive products. Similarly the peril point procedure required an investigation prior to any tariff reductions in order to determine the limit to which concessions could be made without causing or threatening serious injury to domestic industries. The task of carrying out these investigations was given to the ITC, a body Congress regarded as one of its fact-finding arms; however, the president was permitted to retain the power to reject the recommendations of the commission.

Initially when the president chose not to adopt the ITC's recommendations, he had only to explain his reasoning to Congress. The pressure that this requirement put on the president to accept ITC affirmative findings apparently proved to be insufficient from the viewpoint of Congress, and the 1958 extension of the Trade Agreements Act introduced a provision that enabled Congress to override by a two-thirds vote presidential decisions rejecting an affirmative escape clause finding. The 1962 and 1974 Trade Acts reduced the required vote for a congressional veto, first to a majority of the authorized membership of each house and then to just a majority of those present and voting in each house. Although Congress has never exercised this veto authority, the threat to do so does seem to have influenced the president's trade policy actions toward some industries. In the *Immigration and Naturalization Service* v. *Chadha* decision in 1983, however, the Supreme Court declared that all such congressional veto provisions were unconstitutional because they violated the presentment clauses of the Constitution. The Court's basic argument was that the legislative veto was essentially legislative in purpose and effect and that all such legislative actions had to be approved by both the House and Senate and presented to the president, as are all public and private bills and joint resolutions (except joint resolutions proposing amendments to the Constitution, which require a two-thirds vote of both houses and need not be signed by the president).[8] Consequently in the Trade and Tariff Act of 1984 Congress changed this provision to conform with the Supreme Court decision. The law now states that if the president rejects an affirmative ITC condition, the ITC's recommendation to remedy the injury will take effect if both houses pass a joint resolution disapproving the president's action. This resolution can be vetoed by the president. A two-thirds vote of both houses is required to override the president's veto.

The Trade Expansion Act of 1962 replaced the Trade Agreements Act of 1934 as the basic U.S. authority for undertaking multilateral reductions of trade barriers. Although it gave the president significant additional tariff-cutting power, at the same time it further circumscribed the manner in which he could exercise his import policy powers. The act was, for example, considerably more detailed and precise than earlier laws in describing the objectives to be sought and the procedures to be followed in trade negotiations. The most important change brought about by Congress was to provide for the appointment by the president of a special representative for trade negotiations charged with conducting these negotiations and housed in the Executive Office of the President. Prior to this time, the State Department had chaired the interagency committee that directed all trade negotiations. However, most members of Congress had long felt that State was not sufficiently responsive to the needs of domestic industries, and they hoped that by designating a nominee whose confirmation would depend primarily on that person's trade views, the concerns of Congress would be given greater weight. The 1962 law also provided that two members of the House Ways and Means Committee and of the Senate Committee on Finance be appointed as members of the U.S. delegation to each multilateral trade negotiation.

In approving the Trade Act of 1974, Congress took another major step in regaining some of the trade policy powers it had delegated to the president. The act did not just authorize the president to enter into trade agreements dealing with unduly burdensome nontariff trade barriers, as did the 1962 act. It also directed the president to seek revisions of the General Agreement on Tariffs and Trade (GATT) with respect to twelve specific nontariff issues. Most important it required that the president consult with members of the Ways and Means and Senate Finance committees, as well as other relevant congressional committees, before entering into nontariff trade agreements and to submit these agreements for approval to both houses of Congress. Other provisions in the 1974 law that aimed at increasing the influence of Congress and other groups over trade policy included increasing the congressional membership in any U.S. delegation negotiating trade agreements to five from each house, establishing an elaborate set of advisory committees from the private sector, reorganizing and expanding the powers of the ITC, and stripping the executive branch of control over the budget of the commission.

The Trade Agreements Act of 1979 and the Trade and Tariff Act of 1984 continued these congressional efforts. In the 1979 act the president was directed to submit a plan that would restructure the trade functions of the executive branch and include mechanisms for monitoring and enforcing U.S. rights under all trade agreements.[9] The private advisory committees established for the Tokyo Round of trade negotiations were also continued and their scope extended to include matters relating to the administration of existing trade agreements and to trade policy in general. The 1984 act provides the president specific negotiating authority to reduce or eliminate barriers to trade in services as well as the trade-distortive effects of certain investment-related measures, such as export performance requirements. Furthermore as a means of pressuring the president to take such actions, the U.S. trade representative is required to report annually to Congress on the extent of foreign measures that distort U.S. exports of goods and services and U.S. direct investments abroad, on the actions taken during the year to reduce or eliminate such distortions, and on current plans aimed at doing so.

A rough idea of the increase over the years in the degree of specificity in the authority granted the president can be obtained by noting that the Trade Agreements Act of 1934 was 2 pages long, the 1958 extension 8 pages long, the Trade Expansion Act of 1962, 32 pages, the Trade Act of 1974, 99 pages, the Trade Agreements Act of 1979, 173 pages, and the Trade and Tariff Act of 1984, 102 pages.

Congress has other means besides legislation to exert

influence on trade policy. One well-known method is the review of an agency's performance that takes place as part of the annual budgetary process. Congress can withhold budgetary support for particular administrative activities by the executive branch if it does not approve of the manner in which they are being carried out. The various congressional committees also hold hearings for the purpose of shaping import policies. The House Ways and Means Committee has primary jurisdiction over trade involving import duties, reciprocal trade agreements, and revenue measures generally.[10] The House Committee on Agriculture handles all trade matters relating to agriculture. In addition, such committees as Energy and Commerce; Banking, Finance and Urban Affairs; and Foreign Affairs have jurisdiction over certain aspects of trade policy. A similar situation prevails in the Senate, where the Finance Committee has primary jurisdiction over reciprocal trade agreements and foreign trade but the Committees on Banking, Housing and Urban Affairs; Foreign Relations; Commerce, Science, and Transportation; and Agriculture, Nutrition, and Forestry also deal with trade issues. Other committees without legislative responsibilities, such as the Joint Economic Committee, also schedule hearings on various import issues. Still another effective method by which the Senate affects import policy is through its power to confirm or reject presidential appointments to the departments and agencies dealing with trade matters. The Senate also must approve by at least a two-thirds vote any treaty negotiated by the president.

2.2 Congressional Behavior toward Protectionism

The analytical framework for this study assumes that members of Congress, like other individuals, seek to satisfy their own policy preferences. Since their ability to carry out this goal depends on periodic approval by the voters, legislators must satisfy the policy wishes of their constituents sufficiently to secure and retain their elected positions. Under conditions of perfect knowledge and in the absence of entry barriers into political markets, this implies that legislators will simply carry out the public policy preferences of a majority of voters. But when the various imperfections and rigidities characterizing the actual elective process are introduced, the behavior of those serving in elective bodies like Congress becomes considerably more complex. This section explores in more detail some of these complexities and on the basis of the political-economic framework being utilized elaborates further concerning the likely behavior of individual members of Congress and the Congress as a whole in response to trade policy pressures.

Factors Influencing Trade Policy Decisions
of Members of Congress

The existence of imperfect knowledge and information costs gives rise to the possibility that legislators will support import protection even when such a policy is a nationally inefficient means of allocating resources and redistributing income. The models set forth in chapter 1 suggest that whether a particular member of Congress supports protectionist measures depends mainly on the economic and political characteristics of the district he represents, the policy position of his political party, his relations with his colleagues and the president, and his own social and economic goals. More specifically, a member of Congress is more likely to support protectionist policies: (1) the higher is the proportion of workers in his constituency who are employed in import-sensitive industries and the larger the campaign contributions from workers and management in these industries; (2) the lower is the proportion of workers in his constituency who are employed in industries using the outputs of the injured industries as intermediate inputs and the smaller the campaign contributions from these industries; (3) the lower is the proportion of workers in his constituency who are employed in industries with significant exports or direct investments abroad and the smaller the campaign contributions from these sectors; (4) the less liberal is his political party's position on trade policy; (5) the less opposed is the president (especially when he is a member of the same party) and the congressional leadership of his own party to protectionist policies; (6) if the support for protection for particular industries does not also involve opposition to legislation authorizing a multilateral tariff-reducing negotiation; and (7) the stronger is the case for import protection on the grounds that it is consistent with such widely supported social and economic goals as providing special assistance to low-income, unskilled workers and retaliating against the unfair trade practices of foreign producers.

When import competition leads to unemployment and financial losses in major industries represented by a legislator, not only are a large number of voters hurt directly but a considerable number of other constituents are adversely affected in an indirect manner. These include voters employed in industries supplying intermediate inputs and capital goods to the injured sectors, as well as those who provide consumer goods and services to the injured industries' employees. Furthermore a rise in the unemployment rate reduces local tax revenues in the political units making up the constituency of a person elected to Congress. Consequently when workers and management in the injured industries are well organized for political action and are not only prepared to withhold their voting support from a member of Congress who does not favor protectionist policies aimed at helping these industries but are willing to provide generous financial and manpower support for election purposes for a candidate who will work for enactment of such policies, elected officials will jeopardize their political position unless they behave in a protectionist manner.

There is not likely to be much resistance within such legislative districts to the strong pressures for protecting these industries from import competition. The only sectors for which it might be economically worthwhile to oppose this policy actively are those that use significant amounts of the injured industries' products as intermediate inputs and that would be faced with higher input costs with import protection. If the number of firms in the injured industries is relatively small, however, the intermediate input users will be concerned about the availability of their inputs should the injured industries regain their economic health by means of protection and then punish those firms that were not supportive. Furthermore industrial purchasers of the industries' products are, through their close economic relationships with the injured sectors, likely to be made aware of sympathetic versions of the injured industries' problems and to be led to believe that they too may need protection in the not-too-distant future. Workers and management in other import-competing industries, even though they may be enjoying prosperous conditions, also may support assistance to the injured sectors for this reason.

The existence in the same region of export industries and firms with significant direct investments abroad will tend to restrain congressional candidates from supporting generalized protectionism but not from advocating protection for particular industries. Each export industry will realize that the chances that any foreign retaliation, in response to their country's withdrawal of tariff concessions on a few import-injured industries, will affect their particular exports are very slight. Thus they usually will not actively oppose protection for such industries.[11] Export industries will, however, urge their congressional representatives to work for export-assisting measures such as tax breaks and below-market borrowing rates, as well as for a reduction in foreign import barriers. Since the reduction of these barriers is generally tied to the rounds of GATT-sponsored multilateral trade negotiations, they will exert political pressure on their legislators to support multilateral trade negotiations and to oppose general protectionism, which jeopardizes these negotiations. Export industries, however, are likely to be in better economic condition than import-competing sectors, and the relationship between support for a multilateral trade negotiation and gaining export benefits for any particular industry is very indirect. Thus counterpressures from export industries are not likely to match the intensity of the protectionist pressures exerted by import-competing sectors suffering from low profits and high unemployment rates. First-hand knowledge about the economic plight of the import-injured workers is also likely to weaken the local opposition from internationally oriented public interest groups.

Export interests and public interest groups are effective in countering pressures for trade restrictions by import-competing industries in which there are not significant unemployment or profit problems. Although management and labor in any sector will always seek higher profits and more jobs, the pressures for protection will be much weaker from firms enjoying historically satisfactory (in terms of survival) profit and employment levels than from those suffering economic losses. It is difficult to organize a firm's workers into an effective pressure group on either self-interest or altruistic grounds if no jobs have been lost or are threatened. The general public also will not be supportive of protection for such industries on these grounds. Furthermore when new productive capacity is needed to take full advantage of an increase in protection, each firm will be uncertain as to the degree that the firm versus its competitors will benefit from the restriction of imports. When excess capacity already exists in the industry, each firm knows that it can compete immediately for the increased demand for domestic production.

Members of Congress representing districts with some small industries facing severe competition from foreign producers are not likely to push as vigorously for the protection of these sectors as they would for large industries in their districts. Small industries usually do not possess sufficient voting strength or contribute enough campaign funds to warrant a major effort to secure protection. Not only must elected officials allocate their scarce time so that their principal pressure groups are satisfied, but they know that it is almost impossible to obtain protection for a small industry by means of legislation directed solely to that end. On the other hand, because these industries are small, pledges to support protection are also less likely to attract the attention of those who are concerned about the spread of this policy. Consequently members of Congress will tend to support tariff assistance for these industries but will not seek industry-specific protection in a vigorous manner. They may well introduce such legislation to register their support for their constituents, but if they do any more, it will be to concentrate their protectionist efforts on broad legislative provisions that make it easier for small industries to be granted import relief through such procedures as petitioning the ITC.

When the number of voters allegedly injured by import competition in the area represented by a member of Congress is small and there are not significant intermediate-use sectors or export interests concerned about the adverse effects of protection, the members' political position on import issues usually will not affect their chance of reelection to any appreciable degree. Some voters will still wish to assist workers in adversely affected industries on insurance or equity grounds, even though these workers reside outside the district, and others will support trade liberalization for self-interest consumption or general public policy reasons. However, as various studies of constituency behavior have indicated (Fenno 1978; Mayhew 1974; Froman 1963), most voters will not pay much attention to the legislator's vote on these issues or even make an effort to determine the elected official's voting record.

A number of different factors can influence the behavior of members of Congress in this situation. If members are under considerable constituency pressure to demonstrate their policy effectiveness on some other issue, they may use their vote on trade policies as a bargaining device to gain the support of other colleagues for the position they favor on this other issue. Other alternatives are to adopt the policy position of some public interest group that can be helpful in their reelection efforts or simply to be guided by the social and economic goals they wish to promote themselves. For example, if they are greatly concerned about improving the income position of the least skilled and poorest groups in the labor force, they may favor import protection for such unskilled labor-intensive industries as apparel but not for such high-wage industries as steel. But if the difficulties of the steel industry are due to dumping and subsidization by foreign producers, their concerns about unfair import practices may cause them to support protection for this industry too. Other goals that may condition the behavior of a member of Congress include a desire to promote domestic economic growth, reduce inflation, assist the developing nations, maintain a particular way of life, and provide an adequate industrial structure for national defense purposes.

Because of the extensive knowledge that is often needed about an issue to assess accurately the consistency of a particular policy stance with a legislator's broad social goals, many members of Congress may, as Kingdon (1973) and Mathews and Stimson (1975) explain, follow the voting behavior of those in Congress who are especially knowledgeable in trade matters and who share their general political and social views. Usually this consensus or cue-taking mode of decision making involves consulting with members of their own party who serve on the key committees dealing with trade issues and thus who tend to implement the party's trade policy objectives. This type of behavior enables members to devote more of their time to matters of greater concern to their constituents and also tends to ensure that their votes will be consistent with the general social and economic stances they want to promote and be known for among their constituents. Furthermore by seeking to join with fellow party members on relevant committees, their reputation as a team player is enhanced within Congress and with this their personal standing in Congress.

Still another behavior pattern some members of Congress may follow when import competition is not an important constituent or interest group issue in their districts is to use their behavior on trade issues to create a reputation that will appeal to their electorates or increase their influence within Congress. To do this effectively, the member must usually be on a committee dealing with trade issues, since it provides both a forum and a relatively easy opportunity to acquire expertise in the field. Members of Congress may, for example, try to acquire a reputation among their constituents of seeking to remove bureaucratic red tape from exporting or of defending U.S. industry and labor from unfair foreign trade practices. Although industry and labor in their districts may not be especially concerned about exports or imports, these voters are likely to admire the legislators' efforts to promote the nation's general welfare. The optimum committee assignment is one where the legislator can further the direct economic interest of constituents and build up a good public policy image. Consequently it would be expected that legislators from districts where trade issues, especially import competition, are of considerable concern to constituents would seek membership on committees dealing with those issues.

Seeking the respect and admiration of colleagues not only contributes directly to legislators' job satisfaction but brings rewards that enable them to serve these constituents more effectively.[12] For example, when legislators become expert in some aspect of the governmental processes under the jurisdiction of their committees, they not only gain the satisfaction of being consulted, but the interests of their constituents are likely to be given greater weight by the congressional leadership and colleagues.

The views of the president also influence the trade policy behavior of members of Congress, especially those who belong to the same political party as the president. This influence will be particularly strong when the issue under consideration is a major trade proposal of the president, such as a new round of multilateral trade negotiations. In such cases it is very important for a president's domestic and international political prestige for him to succeed in getting Congress to accept the basic elements of his proposal. Consequently he often exerts political pressure on a member by utilizing his ability to influence the probability of the member's reelection through promises of personal campaign visits, federal appointments to key constituents, and federal government expenditures in the district. Those who belong to the same party as the president tend to be more receptive to this pressure, but other members will also be affected by it.

The reaction of members of Congress to a proposed multilateral duty-cutting negotiation is also likely to be somewhat different than to pressures for protection from particular industries in their districts or states at other times. A general duty-cutting negotiation appeals to voters on the grounds that it promotes economic prosperity in other countries and also contributes to general U.S. prosperity and international political stability. Consequently members of Congress who oppose legislation authorizing such a negotiation risk the loss of some political support due to their perceived opposition to desirable foreign policy objectives. In districts where employment in import-sensitive industries is significant, the typical legislator will generally rank the immediate economic interests of this group above the collective goal of improving foreign relations and therefore oppose the liberal trade legislation. Sometimes, however, these industries are able to gain a promise of no-duty cuts (or only minimal ones) from the administration prior to a vote on the legislation. Under these circumstances, members of Congress heavily dependent on the support of such industries for reelection are likely to vote for the trade-liberalizing legislation. Furthermore legislators who represent areas where import-sensitive industries are less important politically are also likely to vote for the legislation with the promise to these industries that they will work to reduce the cuts to which they will be subject.

In addition to the various influences mentioned thus far, investigators of congressional behavior have found that such diverse factors as the competitiveness of an elected official's district, the length of time the member has been in office, and the geographic area in which the district is located also effect voting and other congressional behavior patterns. As Fiorina (1974) points out, however, the relationships found by various investigators between voting behavior and these factors are weak and fluctuate considerably over time. Consequently no attempt is made to include them in the statistical analysis of congressional voting behavior on trade policy undertaken in section 2.3 of this chapter.

Implementing Trade Policy Objectives in the House and Senate

The task members of Congress face in trying to obtain legislative protection against imports that compete with industries in their districts is formidable. If an industry has lobbying muscle in only a few districts, a legislator will have to join with other legislators in seeking protection for the industries they wish to help. As the number of industries covered increases in order to generate more support, so does the opposition. Those representing export interests become more concerned about the possibility that foreign retaliation will cause injury to their industries. Colleagues and the congressional leadership become increasingly apprehensive over the possibility that the party will lose votes for favoring special interest groups. Finally, the president is likely to veto a bill that specifically protects a number of industries, since his election is highly dependent on promoting national goals that appeal to the most voters. When a sector is politically important in many districts and states, as textiles and agriculture are, a member's chances of obtaining legislation that protects it are much more favorable.

Because of these difficulties, most members of Congress seek the enactment of general trade policy rules that might help the industries in which they are especially interested. For example, a legislator who believes that foreign subsidization or dumping is part of the cause of constituents' injuries will push for a tightening of U.S. antisubsidization and antidumping laws. Not only does this procedure enable members to promote the interests of different industries in an unobtrusive manner, but it enables the group to appeal for support on grounds that are widely accepted as desirable for the nation: protecting industry and labor from unfair foreign competition.

The members of Congress likely to have the greatest influence over import issues are those who serve on the committees with relevant legislative authority, principally the Ways and Means Committee in the House and the Finance Committee in the Senate. The legislative authority of these committees and the expertise members acquire about trade issues (especially those serving on the trade subcommittees of these broader committees) give them leadership roles in the field. These roles are especially important when the specifics of trade legislation proposed by the president are being worked out with the executive branch. The chairpersons of the committees, who have the power to schedule meetings and shape agendas, are particularly influential. Although their authority ultimately depends on the support of their colleagues, the political marketplace in Congress, as elsewhere, is far from perfect, and these individuals are sometimes able to secure protective assistance for particular industries of interest to them that other members of Congress would be unable to obtain. Chairpersons of other major committees and the formal leaders of the House and Senate can also use their powers to block or shape legislation on matters outside the trade area to obtain the support of their colleagues or the executive branch for protecting specific sectors of concern to them. However, although committee chairpersons may be able to obtain preferential treatment in their own branch of Congress, this favoritism may not hold up in the other house unless the industries have strong support from key leaders there too.

The differences in size, constitutional functions, and rules governing behavior between the two houses of Congress also influence the type of trade legislation emerging from each body. The rules of the Senate constrain individual behavior far less, both within committees and on the floor itself, than is the case in the House. Consequently it is more difficult for the leadership to turn aside the wishes of senators than individual members of the House. In addition, it is easier for senators to set forth their views before the whole body (and even to filibuster), as well as to negotiate personally with a majority of other senators. In turn it is thus easier for them to gain the support of a significant number of colleagues and to obtain concessions from committee chairpersons. The procedural rules in the House are designed to bring order to the deliberations of such a large body and especially to prevent logrolling from getting out of hand.[13] This situation makes it more difficult for industries other than large ones with considerable political influence or a significant number of representatives to be singled out for special protection. As a result, a larger number of the import-affected industries that are not represented by significant electoral strength in Congress are likely to be singled out for protection in Senate legislation than in bills coming out of the House.

There is also a greater feeling of collegiality among Senate than House members that is due to the Senate's smaller size and more liberal rules on behavior. This characteristic tends to make individual senators identify with Congress itself to a greater degree than do individual members of the House. Senators are therefore usually more jealous of their constitutional authority in relation to that of the executive and judiciary branches than are House members. Consequently it can be expected that the Senate will be more interested in exercising the trade powers of Congress and especially in trying to prevent the president from assuming too many of these powers.

An opportune time for members of Congress to implement their import policy objectives is when a president is seeking the enactment of a particular piece of trade legislation. They can count on the willingness of most presidents to compromise extensively on their initial proposals rather than fail to obtain any legislation at all. On these occasions, it is easiest to obtain protectionist changes in the general rules established for implementing trade policy, such as the criteria for granting import relief, as well as modifications in the trade laws that implement some nontrade goal, such as a reduction in the power of the president. Furthermore industries capable of mobilizing significant voting blocs in Congress or of securing the support of key congressional leaders can often at this time obtain immediate, industry-specific relief through executive branch action outside of a particular piece of legislation. How effective protectionist interests will be on these occasions depends not only on such obvious factors as the president's party strength and popularity in Congress but also on how successful he has been in selling his nationally oriented political and economic reasons for requesting trade legislation. Voter concern for social welfare not only encompasses matters of domestic equity but also such international considerations as national defense, international prestige, and national competitiveness. The furtherance of goals such as these at times may take precedence in voters' minds over a desire to assist those allegedly injured by import competition.

Although occasions when the president is proposing major new trade legislation are especially opportune times for Congress to implement its trade policy goals, this body also has considerable influence in shaping trade policy at other times. One method by which Congress exerts this influence is to hold hearings on the trade problems of particular industries and on the alleged unfair trade practices of other countries as a means of generating support among other legislators and the public in general for some restrictive trade policy action. Then by threatening to initiate legislative action itself or to block some nontrade-related measure desired by the president, Congress can sometimes force the president to act in the desired manner under powers he already possesses.

2.3 Formulating and Implementing the Trade Act of 1974

Many of the behavior patterns discussed in the preceding section and in chapter 1 can be illustrated or tested by considering the import policy actions of Congress during the five-year period extending from the formulation of the Trade Act of 1974 to the enactment in 1979 of legislation implementing the multilateral trade negotiations held under the authority granted the president in the 1974 act.

Modifying the Administration Bill

In early 1973 the Nixon administration requested broad trade policy authority from Congress in order to conduct a new round of multilateral trade negotiations. The bill introduced at the administration's request would have permitted the president to modify tariffs up or down to any degree he determined appropriate when negotiating with other countries. In addition the bill would have granted him the authority necessary to conclude international agreements on nontariff trade measures. If he determined it was appropriate or necessary to submit these nontariff agreements to Congress, either house would have to act within ninety days. Unless either house disapproved the measure by a majority vote within the ninety days, the measure would take effect. The time limit for these various powers was five years. There was, however, to be an ongoing authority with respect to modest trade agreements and the raising or lowering of duties by no more than 20 percent.

These requests turned out to be unrealistic politically. Not only did the strong protectionist attitudes that developed in Congress after the completion of the Kennedy Round of trade negotiations in 1967 still prevail, but many members of Congress believed that the power of the president in the trade field was already too great. The Nixon administration also failed to undertake a major effort to convince the general public of the importance of its proposals on grounds of national interest, as the Kennedy administration had done with its 1962 proposals. Because of these factors, the bill was substantially modified by both houses of Congress. The House passed its own trade bill on December 12, 1973, while the Senate did not adopt its own bill until December 13, 1974. A compromise version of both bills was adopted on December 20, 1974.

Both houses rejected the president's request for complete discretion to alter duties, though the final duty-cutting power granted the chief executive was significant. The original House bill would have allowed duties above 25 percent to be cut by 75 percent (but not below 10 percent), duties greater than 5 but less than 25 percent by 60 percent, and duties of 5 percent or less by 100 percent. The bill passed by the Senate permitted a 50 percent cut on rates of 10 percent or more and a 100 percent reduction on duties below 10 percent. The final act allowed 60 percent cuts above the 5 percent duty level and 100 percent reductions for rates 5 percent or less. Congress accepted five years as the time frame for this trade-negotiating authority but limited the period for concluding further modest agreements to two years.

Even more significant changes were made concerning the president's authority to negotiate modifications in nontariff, trade-distorting measures. In place of the general language of the administration bill, the House stated that the president's negotiators should use the sector approach to obtain for U.S. exports to other developed countries competitive opportunities equivalent to those afforded in the United States. They were also to seek reform of the GATT in several specific areas, including the decision-making machinery, safeguards against injurious import increases, government procurement, fair labor standards, and border tax adjustments. The Senate bill added export controls, subsidies, and the most-favored-nation principle to this list, stressed that access to supplies should be a principal negotiating objective, and directed the president to seek a footwear agreement in the GATT similar to the one in existence for textiles. The final bill combined these various directives to the president, although the one dealing with the footwear agreement was made less definitive.

The key modification was that the Congress did not accept just a veto right over the nontariff agreements. While the House did accept the president's proposal, although requiring the negotiators to consult with the Ways and Means and Senate Finance Committees before entering into agreements, the Senate did not. The views of the Senate, where pressures to reduce the powers of the president in trade matters have been strongest, prevailed. Not only was consultation with relevant congressional committees required before entering into agreements covering non-tariff issues, but all such agreements, together with the necessary changes in domestic legislation, had to be ap-

proved by both houses of Congress before they would become effective. Congress, however, was not allowed to
amend the implementing bill and was required to vote on
it within ninety legislative days.

In asking for broad negotiating authority, the administration proposed several changes in the existing trade law
that it apparently believed were sufficiently appealing that
Congress would accept them without significant amendment. These related to the requirements for obtaining
import relief, to antidumping and countervailing duty
procedures, to trade procedures for safeguarding the balance of payments, and to unfair trade practices. In addition, as a means of carrying out his foreign policy
goals, the president requested authority to grant tariff
preferences to developing countries and, subject to the
ninety-day congressional veto procedure, to extend most-
favored-nation treatment to countries not receiving it.

Congress also made substantial changes to these proposals. The administration's import relief proposal, for example, would have eliminated the need for a connection
between previous concessions and import injury, making
it necessary only for imports to be "the primary cause" of
serious injury rather than, as the 1962 act stipulated, "the
major factor." The House and final versions of the bill
required that imports be only "a substantial cause" of serious injury for import relief to be granted. A provision for
the congressional override of presidential rejections of
affirmative findings by the ITC also was included, contrary
to administration wishes, and was even loosened in comparison with its 1962 form. The 1962 stipulation that in
affirmative cases the commission find the amount by
which the duty or other form of restriction should be
changed to remedy the serious injury was also reinserted
by the Congress.

With respect to adjustment assistance for displaced

workers, the administration proposed that the criteria for eligibility be eased so that increased imports need only to have "contributed substantially" to unemployment rather than to have been "the major factor" causing the unemployment. The Congress weakened the criteria even further by substituting "contributed importantly" for the administration's terminology. As the report of the Ways and Means Committee noted, the term *substantial* means a cause that is not only important but not less than any other cause. The term *important* does not require this last condition, and it is so stated in the final act.

The main change in the antidumping and countervailing duty areas proposed by the administration was to fix time limits on both types of investigations. The secretary of the treasury was also given the option of not applying countervailing duties if he determined they would be detrimental to U.S. economic interests or if existing quantitative restrictions were adequate. Congress added to this a fast track procedure for handling dumping cases and, in an action that subsequently became very important for the multilateral trade negotiations, limited the authority of the secretary of the treasury to waive the imposition of countervailing duties to a four-year period, providing there was progress in the negotiations on GATT reform in this area.

The provisions the president requested with regard to unfair trade practices were by and large accepted by Congress, as were those dealing with the balance of payments, except that the maximum level of the permitted import surcharge was set at 15 percent. The House modified the broadly phrased administration request on tariff preferences by specifying the list of countries to be excluded; the Senate then expanded this list and added certain product exclusions. These exclusions, all of which remained in the final act, covered textile and apparel products subject to textile agreements, watches, import-sensitive electronic and steel articles, footwear, and import-sensitive semi-manufactures and manufactured glass products.[14] The other major part of the administration's trade bill—the power to grant most-favored-nation treatment to communist countries—became the focal point of an effort to lower emigration barriers in the Soviet Union.[15] The final act constrained the president from granting export credits and most-favored-nation treatment to nonmarket economies unless the country permits its citizens to emigrate without heavy taxes.

Besides radically changing a number of the administration's proposals, Congress took the opportunity to regain more control over trade policy by implementing certain trade policies the president had not touched on at all. The most important was reorganizing the ITC (including the change of name from the Tariff Commission) and giving this body expanded powers, including the right to issue cease-and-desist orders in cases of unfair import practices, as well as greater independence from the executive branch. The power of the executive was also somewhat reduced by establishing a mechanism for bringing the private sector into the negotiations in more formal ways than before.

In summary, the legislative history leading up to the passage of the Trade Act of 1974 is consistent with a number of the hypotheses suggested in chapter 1 and in this chapter. One clearly supported theme emphasized by Pastor (1980) as well as Cohen and Meltzer (1982) is the importance of the interactions between the president and Congress in shaping modern trade policy. The manner in which Congress modified the administration's proposal signaled an end to the view that trade policy was mainly a foreign policy matter and therefore largely the prerogative of the president. Important changes were made that required the president to share to a greater extent the responsibility of implementing trade policy. The interactions between the Congress and the president that occurred also support the view that an opportune time for Congress to exercise influence on trade policies is when the president is seeking a major new international initiative in the field. Still another theme substantiated by the events of this period is the autonomous nature of some actions by the state. Certain provisions introduced into the Trade Act of 1974 by Congress seem to be more the result of Congress's view of the proper relationship between the executive and legislative branches of government than the consequence of any well-defined constituency interest.

A comparison between the president's proposals and the modifications introduced by Congress also supports the hypothesis that the president is more liberal on trade matters than the Congress. As expected, within the Congress the House concentrated on enacting general provisions that provided greater import protection whereas the Senate singled out a larger number of specific industries for special import assistance. Furthermore the actions of both the Congress and the president with respect to trade adjustment assistance, as well as foreign subsidization and dumping, support the view that government agents are responsive to social concerns relating to adjustment problems and equity considerations. The granting of zero-duty treatment to manufacturing exports from developing countries also indicates that equity concerns at the international level can influence government behavior, although foreign policy considerations also played a major role in this decision.

Analysis of the Congressional Vote
on the Trade Act of 1974[16]

The vote in the House on the bill reported out by the Ways and Means Committee was 272 in favor and 140 opposed. The chances for passage had been greatly improved not only because of the various protectionist features accepted by the president during the legislative process but because the administration negotiated a multilateral agreement (the Multifiber Arrangement) permitting quantitative restrictions on all textile and apparel products and renewed the quota arrangement on specialty steel. The effect of the new textile arrangement was dramatic. During the House hearings on the bill in June 1973, industry and labor representatives from the textile and apparel sectors had testified against it, urging passage instead of a generalized quota bill. By the time the House voted on the bill in December 1973, however, the success of the textile negotiations appeared assured, and members of Congress from textile and apparel districts supported the bill. Moreover, when the Senate held its hearings in 1974, representatives from the industry did not even bother to testify, and senators from textile states voted in favor of it.

Of the 140 members of the House who opposed the final act, 121 were Democrats and 19 Republicans.[17] Democratic opposition was centered in the northern states; only 17 of the 149 Democrats representing these states voted for passage of the bill. Not only were several import-sensitive industries located in this region, including footwear, electronics, and steel, but the influence of the AFL-CIO, which opposed the bill, was significant there. The impact of the Multifiber Arrangement was evident from the fact that in the southern textile states of Alabama, Georgia, Mississippi, North Carolina, South Carolina, Tennessee, and Virginia, every Republican and all but two Democrats voted in favor of the bill. The small Republican vote against the bill was composed of a few hard-core protectionists and House members from districts in which import-sensitive industries were located.

The Senate passed its version of the bill seventy-seven to four. A better indication of the relative strength of the protectionist and liberal trade forces than these figures is the vote on an amendment prohibiting the president from cutting duties on manufactures for which the import penetration ratio (imports as a proportion of the domestic market) exceeded one-third in three of the last five years. This amendment failed to pass by a vote of thirty-five to forty-nine, with twenty-six Democrats and nine Republicans favoring it and twenty-three Democrats and twenty-six Republicans opposing it. The states in which both senators favored the amendment were Alabama, Alaska, Indiana, Maine, Massachusetts, Missouri, Pennsylvania, Rhode Island, Virginia, and Washington. Such industries as textiles, shoes, steel, glass, and forestry are important in these states.

An effort to determine in a more formal manner the influence on congressional votes that industries either opposing or favoring trade liberalization have had was undertaken by relating the proportion of the industrial labor force in each congressional district or state employed in import-sensitive and export-oriented industries to the voting behavior of House members and senators on trade bills passed in the House and Senate. If workers or management in an industry testified at the hearings that they opposed tariff liberalization, the industry was classified as import sensitive, whereas if members of the industry expressed support for the bill's liberalized features, the industry was termed export oriented. Table 2.1 lists the import-sensitive sectors. Only two industries—office and computing equipment (SIC 357) and aircraft (SIC 372)—were identified as export oriented.

One drawback to such a list is that it does not take into account the varying intensity of opposition or support for the bill. Automotive workers, for example, seemed to oppose the bill less strongly than electronic workers. Moreover the list itself is partly dependent on the investigator's

Table 2.1
Import-sensitive industries, 1973 House and 1974 Senate hearings

Standard industrial classification (SIC) number	Industry
103	Lead and zinc ores
11	Anthracite coal
12	Bituminous coal and lignite mining
131	Crude petroleum and natural gas
141	Dimension stone
145	Clay, ceramic, and refractory materials
2022	Cheese
2084	Wines, brandy, and brandy spirits
2085	Distilled, rectified, and blended liquors
2432	Veneer and plywood
26	Paper and allied products
2815	Cyclic intermediates, dyes, organic pigments, and cyclic products
282	Plastic materials and synthetic resins
302	Rubber footwear
31	Leather and leather products (includes nonrubber footwear)
321	Flat glass
325	Structural clay products
3262	Vitreous china
3263	Fine earthenware
331	Blast furnaces and basic steel products
3321	Gray iron foundries
3332	Primary smelting and refining of lead
3333	Primary smelting and refining of zinc
342	Hand and edge tools, excluding machine tools
345	Screw machine products
3554	Paper industries machinery
3562	Ball and roller bearings
365	Radio and television sets
366	Communications equipment
367	Electronic components and accessories
371	Motor vehicles
375	Motorcycles, bicycles, and parts
387	Watches, clocks, and parts
391	Silverware, plated ware, stainless steel ware
3941	Games and toys
3942	Dolls
3964	Needles, pins, hooks and eyes, etc.

judgment. A case in point is that the textile and apparel industries were not included in the list of import-sensitive industries, since by the time the House and Senate voted on the bills, the industry's initial negative position had become positive because of the new international textile agreement. In view of these factors, regressions were run on individual industries, as well as on the entire groups of opposition and supporting industries, respectively.

Estimates of the relative importance in each congressional district and each state of those workers employed in import-sensitive and export-oriented industries are based on data from *County Business Patterns, 1973*, and the *Congressional District Data Book, 93rd Congress*, both published by the Bureau of the Census.[18] The voting behavior of members of Congress was not only related to these variables but also to the members' party affiliations and the campaign contributions they received from three major labor unions opposing the bill. (It was not feasible to identify contributions from management on an industry basis.) Since the bill was introduced by a Republican president, it would have been expected that Republican members of Congress would have tended to support the bill. Similarly the likelihood of a negative vote should have increased with an increase in campaign contributions from protectionist unions.[19]

The manner in which a member of Congress voted on the trade bill or, in the case of the Senate, an amendment to the bill is the dependent variable in the probit analysis reported in tables 2.2 and 2.3. A "yes" or pro-liberal trade vote was assigned the number 0, while a negative or protectionist vote was assigned a 1. For the party affiliation variable (one of the independent variables), membership in the Republican party was assigned a 1 and membership in the Democratic party a 0. Since Republicans should have tended to favor the bill and Democrats to oppose it, a nega-

Table 2.2
1973 House vote on the trade bill related to various economic and political factors

Variable	Equation 1	Equation 2	Equation 3
Constant	−.40 (2.78)**	−.25 (1.50)	−.23 (1.17)
Party affiliation	−1.20 (6.79)**	−1.24 (6.95)**	−1.45 (6.95)**
Union contributions	.0004 (3.22)**	.0004 (2.89)**	.0003 (2.11)*
Import-sensitive industries	3.49 (2.62)**	3.28 (2.45)**	.76 (.17)
Export-sensitive industries	1.16 (1.28)	−.11 (.03)	−3.38 (1.92)*
Textiles and apparel		−2.46 (1.64)	16.51 (2.35)**
Oil and coal			112.08 (3.19)**
Screw machine products			44.87 (2.11)*
Watches, silverware, games, dolls, and needles			−62.62 (2.15)*
Hand tools			102.47 (1.75)
Coal tar products			32.45 (.18)
Lead and zinc			−3604.58 (.22)
Ceramic materials			42.57 (.73)
Cheese			−76.30 (.67)
Wines and liquors			−58.22 (.13)
Veneer and plywood			5.09 (.64)
Paper			−15.97 (.92)
Plastics			−66.15 (1.06)
Rubber footwear			13.51 (1.21)
Leather products			26.45 (.61)
Flat glass			

Clay and china products		9.15	(.24)
Basic steel and iron		2.29	(.73)
Paper machinery		25.74	(.20)
Ball bearings		59.50	(.88)
Electrical equipment		1.13	(.21)
Motorcycles and bicycles		1.06	(.46)
Motor vehicles		−95.03	(.99)
(−2) time log likelihood ratio	95.68	95.56	138.19

Notes: The *t* statistics are in parentheses in the columns next to the estimated coefficients. By the chi-square test, equations 1 and 2 are significant at the 1 percent level and equation 3 at the 5 percent level.
*Significant at the 5 percent level.
**Significant at the 1 percent level.

Table 2.3
1974 Senate vote on the trade bill related to various economic and political factors

	Equation 1		Equation 2	
Constant	−.72	(2.18)*	−.90	(2.51)**
Party	−.66	(2.21)*	−.66	(2.18)*
Import-sensitive industries	9.71	(2.85)*	9.62	(2.82)**
Export-sensitive industries	10.44	(.91)	13.71	(1.15)
Textiles and apparel			3.92	(1.40)
(−2) times log likelihood ratio	15.75		17.71	

Notes: The t statistics are in parentheses in the columns next to the estimated coefficients. By the chi-square test, equations 1 and 2 are significant at the 5 percent level.
*Significant at the 5 percent level.
**Significant at the 1 percent level.

tive sign is expected on the partial coefficient relating voting and party membership; that is, the higher is the number representing the political party, the lower is the number representing the voting position of a member of Congress. On the other hand, the relationship between the vote on the bill and both the proportion of a district's or state's labor force in import-sensitive industries opposed to the bill and the magnitude of campaign contributions from protectionist unions (two other independent variables) should be positive; that is, the higher is the proportion of those opposed to the bill and the greater are the campaign contributions, the higher is the expected number assigned to depict voting behavior. The relationship between the last independent variable—the proportion of the labor force in industries supporting the bill—and voting behavior should be negative, however.

Equations 1 through 3 in table 2.2 indicate the results of the probit analysis. Equation 1 aggregates all the opposition industries and the two supporting industries. The coefficients on the variables for party affiliation, union contributions, and proportion of workers in import-sensitive industries all have the expected sign and are significant at the 1 percent level. The two export industries do not show up as significant and have the wrong sign. These results support the hypothesis that export-oriented industries are not likely to be as vigorous in their support of liberal trade policies as are import-sensitive sectors in their opposition to this policy.

Equation 2 differs from equation 1 in that the textile and apparel industries have been added. The fact that the coefficient on this term is negative (and almost significant at the 10 percent level) is further evidence that the traditionally protectionist textile sector was persuaded to change its views because of the successful negotiation of a multilateral marketing agreement covering all major textile products.

When the various industries are entered separately (equation 3), the coefficients generally are not significant. Besides textiles and apparel, other industries entering at levels of significance of 5 percent or less are oil and coal, screw machine products, hand tools (with the wrong sign), and a miscellaneous industry group representing watches, games and toys, silverware and stainless steelware, and needles and fasteners. Most of these industries have actively worked for protectionist measures for many years.

The measure selected to test the influence of economic and political factors on voting behavior in the Senate was an amendment by Senator Thomas McIntyre, Democrat from New Hampshire, that would have prohibited the president from reducing tariffs on manufactured goods for which imports exceeded one-third of domestic consumption during three of the last five years. Data on campaign contributions by the three unions were not collected in the Senate; thus the independent variables are party affiliation and the proportion of workers in each state employed in industries either opposing or supporting the administration's proposals.

The two equations in table 2.3 indicate that, as in the House vote, party affiliation and the proportion of workers opposed to liberalization have the expected sign. Again the proportion of workers in industries favoring liberalization is not significant and has the wrong sign. The textile and apparel industry also has the wrong sign but is not significant.[20]

In summary, not surprisingly, the statistical analysis gives support to the hypothesis that in voting on trade-liberalizing legislation, members of Congress are sensitive to the import-competition problems of industries within their districts. Campaign contributions by protectionist unions are also correlated with voting behavior in the expected directions. These results are consistent with both the common interest and voting machine models outlined in chapter 1; however, the fact that the import-sensitive sectors generally faced adjustment pressures because of import competition, and in many cases employed comparatively high proportions of low-wage, unskilled workers, also makes the results consistent with the status quo and social change models.

Interestingly members of Congress do not seem to be responsive to the wishes of constituent industries that support trade liberalization because of their export orientation. This may be due to less political pressure being exerted by these industries on their representatives and senators or perhaps because of less concern for the workers in these industries on adjustment or equity grounds. Finally, the significant results for the party variable confirm the influence of the president on the voting behavior of members of his own party at a time when he is urging the enactment of a major piece of legislation.

Implementing the Tokyo Round Nontariff Agreements

Several hypotheses set forth in this chapter concerning congressional behavior are also supported by events leading to congressional approval of the nontariff agreements reached with other nations during the Tokyo Round of multilateral trade negotiations that followed passage of the Trade Act of 1974. For example, one again observes the importance of the interactions between the president and Congress for the formation of U.S. international economic policy. In addition, during such a period when the president is particularly vulnerable to congressional pressures, the special political influence of large, well-organized industries and of industries represented by key congressional leaders, especially committee chairpersons, becomes clearly evident. One incident also demonstrates the significance of equity concerns in shaping congressional decisions.

The efforts by the president to extend the period in which he could waive the imposition of countervailing duties illustrate the first two of the above three points. The Trade Act of 1974 gave the president temporary authority not to impose countervailing duties to offset subsidies on foreign exports during the negotiation of new international rules for dealing with subsidies. This particular authority expired on January 4, 1979, one year before the president's general negotiating authority did. Consequently when it became apparent that the negotiations would not be completed before the waiver authority would expire, the president requested Congress to extend this authority. Since countervailing duties of $47 million on about $600 million of imports had in fact been waived, not to do so would have jeopardized the success of the final stages of the Tokyo Round.

Although the Subcommittee on Trade of the Ways and Means Committee held hearings on a waiver bill after the president's request, it did not act on the measure. Consequently during the last few days of Congress, the administration sought to add the waiver provision as an amendment to some other measure under consideration by the House and Senate. In the Senate, the chairman of the Senate Finance Committee, Senator Russell Long, obliged by tying the measure to the Sugar Stabilization Act. This bill, as passed by the House, established a domestic sugar price of 15 cents per pound. The Senate Finance Committee earlier had reported favorably on a bill setting the price at 17 cents per pound, but Senator Long, a strong supporter of the industry, reduced the price to 16 cents in an effort to gain acceptance of the bill. Initially his amendment dealing with the countervailing duties issue extended the waiver authority to September 1, 1979. Later, however, he shortened this to February 15, 1979 because those concerned about subsidized steel imports apparently wished to use any further extension of the waiver authority as a means of ensuring that the subsidies code agreed to by U.S. negotiators would be satisfactory from their viewpoint.[21] Both the new sugar price and new termination date for the waiver authority were accepted by the Senate, as was an amendment by Senator Frank Church, Democrat of Idaho and chairman of the Foreign Relations Committee, that authorized the president to contribute 5,000 tons of tin from the national stockpile to the buffer stock of the

International Tin Agreement, as well as to dispose of 30,000 tons on the open market.

The strategy adopted was ingenious and the combination of interest groups impressive.[22] The sugar industry had long been effective in obtaining government assistance, and the fact that Senators Long and Church actively supported the industry's position was of considerable importance. The growing and processing of sugar beets are concentrated in nine states—California, Minnesota, Idaho, Colorado, North Dakota, Washington, Nebraska, Wyoming, and Montana—while sugar cane growing, milling, and refining occur mainly in Florida, Texas, Louisiana, Hawaii, and Puerto Rico. Total employment amounts to about 50,000.

The tin amendment had appeal on two grounds. Contributing to the international tin buffer stock represented a responsible foreign policy action that had been promised previously by the administration. Furthermore, by placing 30,000 tons on the open market, the price of tin would decline, benefiting the tin plate industry, which is part of the steel industry. Finally, by tying the sugar-tin package to the countervailing duty waiver bill, the bill was protected from a presidential veto.

Nevertheless the arrangement eventually broke down. A House-Senate conference committee agreed on a report containing the essentials of the package (though the amount to be received by sugar producers was cut to 15.75 cents and the termination period for waiving countervailing duties extended to August 1, 1979). The Senate accepted the conference report, but the House (where the sugar lobby is not as powerful) did not.

Since European and other participants had refused to complete the trade negotiations unless the waiver authority was extended, the president had given attainment of this authority a very high legislative priority. In the meantime, while importers of products on which countervailing duties had been levied were required to post bonds for the amount of duty, the Treasury did not actually collect the duties.

In the next effort to extend the waiver period, the textile rather than the sugar industry used the occasion to gain additional protection. Unlike the sugar industry, the textile industry had been successful in the waning hours of the last Congress in gaining one of its prime objectives: preventing the president from reducing the tariffs on textile and apparel products in the multilateral trade negotiations. Unfortunately from the industry's viewpoint, the president vetoed this bill.

The textile and apparel industries, which have 2.25 million employees, seem to be the most powerful congressional common interest group in the trade field. Over 200 members of the House served as cosponsors of the bill to prohibit duty reductions on textiles. In the new Congress, the Ways and Means Committee refused to act on the waiver request by the president until the White House had worked out with the industry some satisfactory alternative to the earlier no-duty-cut bill for textiles.[23]

The agreement eventually reached was issued as a White House statement entitled "Administration Textile Program."[24] It began by asserting that the administration "is determined to assist the beleaguered textile and apparel industry and is committed to its health and growth." Among several specific pledges were actions "to tighten controls for the remaining life" of existing agreements under the Multifiber Arrangement, including a restriction on the ability of an exporter to carry over unfilled quotas from one year to the next. The administration also agreed to aim at holding 1979 imports to the 1978 levels when necessary "to preclude further disruption."

After this agreement was announced, a bill extending the waiver authority to September 30, 1979, quickly cleared the Ways and Means Committee by a twenty-eight to one vote and was then approved by the entire House membership. The Senate Finance Committee and the Senate as a whole also promptly passed the bill; however, the chairman of the Congressional Textile Caucus, an official legislative support organization of the House established to promote the economic interests of the industry, in reporting on a briefing the caucus received from textile and apparel representatives, stated: "We plan to watch very carefully to see that this program is carried out. If need be, we will hold the MTN [multilateral trade negotiations] hostage to insure that it is carried out."[25]

The sugar industry also appears to have benefited in the new effort to extend the authority to waive countervailing duties, although it did not obtain the 17 cents per pound figure endorsed earlier by the Senate. Prior to passage of the waiver bill, however, the president agreed to raise the domestic price to 15.8 cents per pound (the world price was about 8.5 cents) by means of increased import fees or, if necessary, by quotas, as well as by a half-cent-a-pound subsidy to farmers. While this did not completely satisfy those in the Senate concerned about the industry, no further attempt was made to tie the waiver bill to a bill for higher sugar prices.

One event connected with the process of implementing the nontariff codes negotiated in the Tokyo Round demonstrates the equity concerns of members of Congress. It concerned the draft code on government procurement policy. Under the code signatories agreed to end the practice of giving domestic producers a price preference over foreign suppliers in bidding on government purchases of nonmilitary goods and services. In the case of the United States, these preferences had amounted to 12 percent for small and minority enterprises (and 6 percent for other U.S. firms) from most federal agencies and 50 percent from the Department of Defense. Although it was anticipated that a number of agencies would be excluded by each signatory from the nondiscriminatory provisions of the code, purchases from small and minority firms were not listed as an exception in the draft code.

This exclusion was pointed out in a speech in the House of Representatives, and several members of Congress subsequently threatened to withhold their support for the entire package of agreements. Their reaction did not appear to be the result of any direct constituent pressure, though the potential for such pressure undoubtedly played a role, but seemed to be based more on the concerns of many members for improving the position of small businesses and the economically disadvantaged. As a result of the objection to the draft code, the president's trade representatives, who are also sensitive to equity considerations (though seemingly not to the extent that members of Congress are), quickly renegotiated the agreement so that it no longer applied "to set-asides on behalf of small and minority businesses." The cost was a further increase in the list of entities excluded by other countries from the code's provisions.

The most significant example of Congress's influence in the implementation process occurred after agreement on most of the draft nontariff codes, as well as on the tariff package, had been reached by the industrial country participants in April 1979.[26] The administration held what amounted to drafting sessions, first with the Ways and Means Committee and then with the Senate Finance Committee, on the Trade Agreements Act of 1979, the implementing bill submitted to Congress. These two committees were given jurisdiction over the bill. Rather than submitting a bill after only informal consultations with interested members of Congress, the administration agreed to the formal markup procedure, providing Congress still another opportunity to shape trade legislation in a situation where the president was vulnerable to industry pressures.

The modifications made in the law with regard to countervailing and antidumping duties illustrate how this opportunity was used. A major change in U.S. trade practices that U.S. negotiators had agreed to accept was the insertion of a "material injury clause" into the U.S. countervailing duty law. According to this clause, a country must, before imposing countervailing duties, not only establish that other countries were subsidizing their exports to the country but that this action was causing material injury to producers in that country.[27] Although Article VI of the GATT already contained a material injury clause, the United States had been excused from introducing one because it was not part of U.S. law at the time the GATT was signed in 1947. As the practice of countervailing against subsidized imports grew in importance, foreign countries began to press strongly for inclusion of an injury clause in U.S. law. At the same time, more and more U.S. industries became convinced that subsidies by foreign governments either were reducing their exports or were causing much of their import competition problems. As a result Congress had instructed the president in the 1974 Trade Act to undertake further negotiations to establish internationally agreed-on rules governing the use of subsidies and the application of countervailing duties. Moreover, as long as these negotiations were proceeding satisfactorily, the imposition of countervailing duties was not required until January 4, 1979.

Several industries, most notably steel, were concerned that the material injury clause would bring about greater import competition. The steel industry is a politically powerful interest group in Congress and was the only other industry besides textiles with its own caucus in the House and Senate.[28] Throughout the debate on extending the waiver authority for countervailing duties, those in Congress, especially the Senate, representing the interests of the industry pressed the administration for a strict definition of the term *subsidy* in the new subsidies code in order to protect this sector further from subsidized imports. They continued these efforts in the markup sessions.

The definition of *subsidy* that emerged in the Trade Agreements Act of 1979 is stricter than in the subsidies code itself. The new domestic law not only covers the list of export subsidies described in an annex of the international code but also a specific list of export subsidies "paid or bestowed directly or indirectly on the manufacture, production, or export of any class or kind of merchandise."[29] These consist of government loans or loan guarantees on terms inconsistent with commercial considerations, goods and services provided at preferential rates by governments, funds granted to cover operating losses, and the assumption of any production costs by government. In contrast to these definitions, the international code is vague on the issue of domestic subsidies and actually cites some of the above measures with the implication that they are legitimate.

The members of the Senate Finance Committee also deleted the word *material* from the Senate version of the injury clause introduced into the U.S. countervailing duties law. The House did not go along with this version, and after Ambassador Robert Strauss insisted that the entire negotiations would collapse without a "material injury" clause, the conference committee accepted the term *material injury*; however, *material injury* was defined weakly in the 1979 act as "harm which is not inconsequential, immaterial, or unimportant."[30] Furthermore when the ITC made a determination on this matter and the votes were divided evenly, the finding was to be considered affirmative.[31] Thus, a two-thirds vote (four of the six commissioners) was needed for a negative finding of material injury, while a 50 percent vote would be sufficient for a positive determination. Moreover, unlike the administration's request in 1973, there was no opportunity for the president to intervene on national interest grounds to prevent the imposition of countervailing duties. That the steel industry was pleased by these various developments was evident from the fact that both the chairman of the Steel Caucus in the Senate, Senator John Heinz, Republican of Pennsylvania, and the American Iron and Steel Institute endorsed the bill.

2.4 Summary

The purpose of this chapter has been to describe Congress's changing role in trade policy formation over the last fifty years, to elaborate on the hypotheses outlined in chapter 1 concerning the behavior of members of Congress on trade policy issues, and to evaluate the extent to which these hypotheses are consistent with events relating to the Tokyo Round of multilateral trade negotiations. The last analysis brings out the complex manner in which constituency interests, the legislative goals of the president and the two political parties, and the policy preferences of members of Congress interact to shape the role of Congress in trade policy formation.

The voting behavior of both the House and Senate on the Trade Act of 1974, as well as the congressional modifications in the bill proposed by the president, are consistent with the hypothesis that Congress is responsive to the competitive problems of import-sensitive industries and labor unions. This responsiveness may be based on a concern for the adjustment and equity problems of such industries, as well as on the lobbying and voting pressures from these sectors. Members of Congress whose districts included high proportions of workers in export-oriented industries did not favor this trade-liberalizing legislative initiative to a significantly greater extent than legislators in districts without such industries.

The evidence also supports the proposition that the president is able to influence the voting behavior of members of his own party on major pieces of legislation such as the Trade Act of 1974. Yet this influence of one branch of government on another is not unidirectional. Congress utilized the desire by the president to undertake a new round of multilateral trade negotiations to introduce provisions in the trade laws that reflected both the concerns of certain constituents about injurious import competition and its own aims relating to the comparative authority of the president and the Congress in implementing trade policies. Compared to what the president recommended, these provisions reflect a more protectionist attitude by Congress, as well as a greater concern for the adjustment and fairness problems faced by import-sensitive industries.

Differences in the behavior of the House and Senate on trade matters are also apparent during the period between 1973 and 1979. The Senate tended to focus more than the House on protective provisions that were industry specific. In addition, the special influence of key committee chairpersons and members of the Ways and Means and Senate Finance committees manifests itself throughout this period.

3　The International Trade Commission

3.1 Introduction

In 1916 Congress established the ITC to provide both it and the president with expert and impartial information for the formulation and implementation of U.S. import policy.[1] As President Woodrow Wilson stated in his congressional message proposing the commission, the objective was to create a body that would be "as much as possible, free from any strong prepossession in favor of any political party and capable of looking at the whole economic situation of the country with dispassionate and disinterested scrutiny."[2] This chapter investigates how closely the commission has followed this apolitical role in carrying out the fact-finding responsibilities assigned to it by Congress.

It was suggested in chapter 1 that because of the length of their terms (nine years) and the impossibility of reappointment, ITC members will not be influenced in their decision making by current economic and political pressures. Instead, it was argued, in seeking personal satisfaction through job performance, commissioners are likely to try to implement closely the economic guidelines established by Congress for making their decisions. There is, however, considerable leeway for decision differences among commissioners because of the general nature of these criteria. The hypothesis suggested was that these differences in decisions will tend to be due mainly to differences in the prior experience and background of the commissioners rather than to ongoing interest group pressures, implying that the nature of the backgrounds of the commissioners will play an important role in the appointment process.

After first briefly reviewing in section 3.2 the manner in which the functions of the ITC have changed since its formation, this chapter elaborates on and tries to test these various hypotheses. Section 3.3 considers in more detail the motivations and behavior of the president and the Congress in the appointment process and examines the extent to which differences in the background of commissioners have influenced the nature of their decisions. The final section first explores more fully the various economic and political factors that might influence commissioners' decisions, and then analyzes the extent to which the commissioners have followed the economic criteria laid down by Congress in reaching their decisions on import relief cases. This analysis also includes an attempt to ascertain whether political pressures from the president, Congress, or private interest groups have influenced these decisions.

3.2 Changing Functions of the Commission

The functions and authority of the commission have varied considerably over its nearly seventy-year history in response to protectionist-versus-liberal trade attitudes in the country and the continuing competition for governmental power between the president and the Congress. At the outset the ITC was simply a general investigatory body whose duty was to investigate such matters as "the administration and fiscal and industrial effects of the customs laws of this country," "the tariff relations between the

United States and foreign countries," "the effect of export bounties and preferential transportation rates," and "effects relating to competition of foreign industries with those of the United States, including dumping and cost of production."[3] A very important feature of the ITC's initial role was that "all information at its command" was to be at the disposal of the president, the House Ways and Means Committee, and the Senate Finance Committee and that it was to make investigations and reports for the president and either of these committees when requested to do so.[4]

The Tariff Act of 1922 expanded the advisory role of the ITC significantly. The president was authorized to increase or decrease import duties up to 50 percent in order to ensure that U.S. tariffs on imported goods equalized the difference in production costs for these goods in the United States and the principal competing country. The ITC was directed to assist the president by undertaking investigations to ascertain these differences in production costs.[5] The commission was given similar investigative and advisory powers with respect to determining instances of unfair import competition and unreasonable or discriminatory practices by foreign countries.[6] In response to these conditions, the president could again increase duties by up to 50 percent or exclude foreign imports.

Although the ITC was reorganized under the Tariff Act of 1930 (the Smoot-Hawley Tariff), its basic functions were not changed. The reorganization resulted from widespread charges that the commission had become politicized and involved the immediate termination of all commissioners' terms (although the president could reappoint the commissioners then in office), as well as a reduction in the term of office from twelve to six years.[7] Not only did the commission retain its previous investigatory and advisory authority with regard to unfair import practices and discriminatory or unreasonable foreign trade practices,[8] but

Chapter 3   82

the act also strengthened its role and that of Congress in
the implementation of the "flexible" tariff provision.[9]
Specifically the act extended to both houses of Congress as
well as to the commission itself the authority to initiate ITC
investigations into differences in costs of production.
Moreover, the ITC was directed to specify the rate changes
needed to equalize production costs. The act also stated
that the president "shall approve these rates . . . if in his
judgment they are necessary to equalize differences in
costs."[10] However, court cases confirmed the authority of
the president to set rates other than those recommended,
as long as he waited for the results of the commission's
investigation.

With the passage of the Trade Agreements Act of 1934,
the formal role of the ITC in determining trade policy declined. The hope that Congress, with the aid of the commission, could engage in detailed tariff rate making in a
manner that would not result in excessive logrolling and
concessions to special interest groups had been destroyed
by the highly protectionist and irrational Smoot-Hawley
Tariff Act of 1930. Thus Congress agreed to carry the flexible tariff notion one step further by delegating to the president the authority to reduce (or increase) duties by up to 50
percent in trade negotiations with other countries. He was,
however, required to seek "information and advice" from
the commission and to obtain similar advice from the Departments of State, Agriculture, and Commerce. The 1934
act explicitly rejected the concept of considering comparative costs of production in negotiating tariff reductions and
exempted all articles included in trade agreements from
the cost equalization provisions of the 1922 and 1930 tariff
acts.

One new authority given to the commission in 1935 was
that of investigating whether quantitative import restrictions are needed to make domestic price support programs

in agriculture effective. The president is required to seek ITC investigations before imposing such restrictions.

The staff of the commission participated actively in the duty reduction process under the reciprocal trade agreements program. Besides having membership on the interagency Trade Agreements Committee (and its various subcommittees) that passed on all recommendations for specific tariff offers and requests prior to their transmission to the secretary of state and the president, experts from the ITC were included on the actual negotiating teams. President Franklin D. Roosevelt also appointed a member of the commission as the first chairman of the committee established to obtain information from interested parties concerning the effect of contemplated trade concessions.

Not until the latter part of the 1940s did the ITC again begin to exercise greater authority in trade policy matters. This took place because of Congress's increasing concern about the injurious effects that the trade liberalization program was having on U.S. industry and about the power of the president in the trade field. Under prodding from Republican members of Congress, in 1947 President Harry S. Truman issued an executive order formalizing the procedures for escape clause actions, that is, the modification or withdrawal of trade agreement concessions in order to remedy serious injury (or the threat of serious injury) to a domestic industry because of greater imports resulting from such concessions. The order also provided for the inclusion of an escape clause in all future trade agreements. A general escape clause had in fact been included in all agreements after 1942, but no public pronouncements on the matter had been made.[11] Finally, the order also replaced the Trade Agreements Committee with the ITC as the investigatory body in escape clause actions. The commission's recommendations were to be considered by the president "in the light of the public interest."[12]

In the 1951 extension of the Trade Agreements Act, Congress formalized the escape clause actions into law and enumerated a list of factors that the commission should consider in determining injury. An investigation was required on request of the president, either house of Congress, the House Ways and Means Committee, the Senate Finance Committee, "any interested party," or the commission itself.[13]

The Trade Acts of 1953 and 1954 did not alter the escape clause to any significant degree; however, the 1955 Trade Agreements Extension Act eased the requirements for serious injury and defined the concept of an industry in a narrower sense. The 1958 act included a provision enabling Congress to override presidential disapprovals of ITC recommendations in escape clause cases.

In extending the trade agreements program in 1948, Congress had included the so-called peril point provision requiring the president to furnish the commission with a list of all products on which he was considering making negotiating concessions. The commission was directed to hold hearings on these concessions and to report to the president the limit of the concessions that could be made on such items without causing or threatening to cause serious injury to domestic industries producing similar products; however, it was left to the president to decide what action to take on the commission's findings.

The ITC's functions under both the escape clause and this peril point provision represented a restoration of some of the authority it had had under the flexible tariff provisions of the 1930 act. Although the peril point provision was repealed in 1949, it was reinserted in the 1951 trade act, as well as in the later renewals during the 1950s. In reintroducing this provision, the Democratic-controlled Congress required the president to report his reasons for not following the commission's recommendations to the

House Ways and Means Committee and the Senate Finance Committee.

One manifestation of the concern of Congress over the powers of the president in trade matters was the prohibition in the 1948 trade act of participation by the commission or its staff in decisions of the committees advising the president on trade agreement matters or negotiations on such agreements. This prohibition was repealed in 1949, but when the peril point provisions were reintroduced in 1951, the ITC voluntarily decided that its staff should not vote on any policy proposals offered in the various trade committees within the executive branch. This practice has continued to the present time.

In 1954 the commission was given the responsibility of determining injury to a domestic industry in cases where the Treasury Department had made a positive finding of dumping under the Anti-Dumping Act of 1921. Prior to this time, Treasury had decided whether dumping and injury had taken place. In 1958 the authority of the ITC in antidumping cases was modified when Congress stipulated that evenly divided votes on injury should be deemed as affirmative determinations.

The 1960s, like the 1930s, was a period in which the power of the commission declined. The escape clause provisions of the Trade Expansion Act of 1962 were made so stringent that the commission did not make a positive finding until 1969. The discouraging effect of the new requirements is indicated by the fact that whereas the ITC had made decisions on ninety-five cases between 1951 and 1962, it issued only twenty-six decisions between 1963 and 1974. The 1962 act also eliminated the peril point provision, and the ITC's role in the initiation of new trade negotiations was only to advise the president "as to the probable economic effects" of modifying import duties. While the broad scope of the negotiations imposed a heavy burden on the commission in carrying out these studies, its recommendations were regarded in much the same way as they had been in the 1930s: as only one input among several used in selecting which products to exclude or cut by less than the 50 percent authority. Another duty assigned the ITC in 1962—determining the products eligible for 100 percent cuts because the exports of the United States and the European Community made up at least 80 percent of world trade—turned out to be inapplicable because of the failure of the United Kingdom to join the community until much later.

The 1962 Trade Act also reduced the role of the ITC in cases of unreasonable or discriminatory practices by foreign countries. The 1922 and 1930 tariff acts had charged the ITC with responsibility for ascertaining whether discriminatory acts against the United States were being practiced and, if so, for bringing them to the attention of the president, together with appropriate recommendations. In restating the authority of the president to take action against discriminatory practices, however, the Trade Expansion Act of 1962 made no mention of an investigatory or advisory role for the commission.[14]

In the mid-1970s there was a significant increase in ITC activity and responsibility. The Trade Act of 1974 made it much easier for a domestic industry to obtain import relief, and many more cases began coming before the ITC.[15] In the first four years of the new legislation, the commission issued thirty-seven decisions, in contrast to only twenty-six during the entire twelve years in which the requirements established by the Trade Expansion Act of 1962 applied. In the next five years, however, 1979 through 1983, the number of decisions decreased to eleven. In sixty percent of the forty-eight cases decided from 1975 through 1983, either the majority of those voting decided in the affirmative or the members split evenly. This contrasts with a figure of only 28 percent for the cases decided under the Trade Expansion Act of 1962.

Although the ITC has played a role since 1922 in cases of unfair import practices, until recently its activities were confined to making recommendations to the president after conducting an investigation. In amending section 337 of the 1930 Tariff Act, the Trade Act of 1974 gave the commission the power to order the exclusion of unfairly traded articles or to issue cease and desist orders with respect to unfair practices. The president can for policy reasons override either of these orders within sixty days of issuance. Between 1962 and 1974, only 12 section 337 cases were handled by the commission, in contrast to 124 from 1975 through 1982.

The ITC was also assigned a role in carrying out the broad new powers given the president in section 301 of the 1974 Trade Act, which is concerned with unfair foreign import restrictions, including unreasonable or discriminatory policies and foreign export subsidies. In taking appropriate steps to eliminate such practices, the president could request the ITC to present its views on the probable economic impact on the United States of any proposed action. Moreover, before the president could act against subsidized exports to the United States, it was necessary both for the Treasury to find the existence of such a subsidy and the commission to determine that the exports had the effect of "substantially reducing sales of the competitive United States product." These latter procedures were made superfluous by the Trade Agreements Act of 1979, which introduced an injury test into the U.S. countervailing duty law. Now duties aimed at offsetting the adverse effects of foreign subsidization can be imposed only if the ITC determines that the subsidized exports have caused material injury to a domestic industry.[16]

As part of the effort to expedite handling of dumping

and subsidization complaints, the commission was directed under the 1979 trade act to make preliminary, in addition to final, determinations of injury. If the preliminary determinations are negative, the investigations are terminated. Between 1980 and 1983, the ITC conducted 140 preliminary antidumping investigations and 127 preliminary countervailing duty investigations.[17] The number of final determinations over this four-year period was 45 for antidumping cases and 41 for countervailing duty cases.

Two additional responsibilities given to the ITC in 1974 are investigations of market disruptions resulting from imports from a communist nation and determinations of the probable economic effects of granting to developing countries duty-free treatment under the Generalized System of Preferences (GSP). The procedures for initiating and carrying out investigations of market disruption (defined as existing when increasing imports are a significant cause of material injury) are the same as those in ordinary import relief cases.[18] Similarly when the president furnishes the commission with a list of articles he is considering for duty-free treatment under GSP, the commission undertakes the same type of investigation as for articles being considered for duty modifications in a multilateral trade negotiation. In 1984 another responsibility was assigned to the commission: to establish a Trade Remedy Assistance Office that on request would provide information to the public concerning remedies and benefits available under the various trade laws and the procedural requirements related to these laws.

The 1974 Trade Act again reorganized the ITC. Its name was changed from the Tariff Commission to the International Trade Commission, and the term of its members was increased from six to nine years. The law stipulated that commissioners could not be reappointed. An automatic system based on seniority was established for determining the chairman and vice-chairman, but this was modified in 1977 to permit the president again to select the chairman.[19] Finally the 1974 act removed the president's control over the commission's budget.

Appeals from ITC decisions are handled by the Court of International Trade and the Court of Appeals for the Federal Circuit. The former court is usually the initial court in which such actions are brought; appeals are taken to the Court of Appeals for the Federal Circuit.[20] The 1979 Trade Act specifies, for example, that negative ITC determinations of material injury in countervailing duty and antidumping cases can be taken to the Court of International Trade, whereas appeals from commission decisions to exclude foreign imports can be brought directly to the Court of Appeals for the Federal Circuit. The U.S. Supreme Court has jurisdiction to consider appeals from decisions of the Court of Appeals for the Federal Circuit but in fact seldom accepts such cases.

3.3 Appointment of Commissioners

The 1916 law establishing the commission specified that it "be composed of six members, who shall be appointed by the president, by and with the consent of the Senate, not more than three of whom shall be members of the same political party."[21] Assessing the manner in which ITC nominations may affect the implementation of his policy goals and election prospects is just one of the hundreds of appointment decisions faced by a president. There seem to be three main factors the White House takes into account in reaching its decisions: the legal constraint concerning the party composition of the commission, the professional experience of prospective nominees, and the political benefits obtained by making a particular nomination.

Party Affiliation Requirement

The stipulation of the 1916 law concerning the political affiliation of ITC members was thought to be necessary because of the highly political nature of trade policy. The Republican party had traditionally pursued a more protectionist policy than the Democratic party, and the framers of the legislation wished to neutralize the influence of any one party; however, there are some obvious ways by which a president might try to avoid the intent of this provision. For example, since some members of both parties hold views on trade policy more similar to the opposition party, a president could nominate only individuals in the opposition party who hold the views of his own party. A second means is simply to delay nominating members of the opposition party and thereby produce a favorable party split on the commission. The president has the option of nominating independents or third-party representatives rather than members of the main opposition party. The classic illustration of this behavior occurred when President Wilson, in appointing the first group of commissioners, selected three Democrats and three Progressives (rather than three Republicans) for the commission.

Evidence of the significance of party affiliation in explaining the voting pattern of commissioners is presented in table 3.1. The voting record of the commissioners on import injury cases is divided into three periods: those that took place between 1949 and 1962, those that were made under the Trade Expansion Act of 1962, and those that occurred between 1975 and 1983 under the Trade Act of 1974. Besides summarizing the voting results for all cases in each of these periods, the table presents the pattern of voting in cases where an affirmative finding was made, as well as in those instances where the decision was either negative or the vote was evenly split.

Table 3.1
Political voting patterns on ITC import injury cases, 1949–1983

	1949–1962				1963–1974				1975–1983			
	Number of cases	Number of votes	Affir-mative	Nega-tive	Number of cases	Number of votes	Affir-mative	Nega-tive	Number of cases	Number of votes	Affir-mative	Nega-tive
			Percentage of votes				Percentage of votes				Percentage of votes	
Affirmative determinations	33				2				26			
Democrats		91	77	33		2	25	75		62	73	27
Republicans		90	94	6		6	100	0		63	94	6
Independents		0	0	0		1	0	100		1	100	0
Negative determinations	58				18				19			
Democrats		158	4	96		47	6	94		43	9	91
Republicans		152	19	81		31	6	94		47	11	89
Independents		0	0	0		16	0	100		3	0	100
Evenly split	8				5				3			
Democrats		17	12	88		13	8	92		8	37	63
Republicans		17	88	12		12	93	7		8	63	37
Independents		0	0	0		1	100	0		0	0	0
All decisions	99				25				48			
Democrats		266	30	70		62	8	92		113	46	54
Republicans		259	50	50		49	37	63		118	58	42
Independents		0	0	0		17	6	94		4	25	75

Except for one cell in the table—the negative determinations for the 1963–1974 period—Republican commissioners always voted in a more protectionist manner than their Democratic or independent counterparts.[22] For example, during the 1949–1962 period Republican members found for injury 50 percent of the times they voted, in contrast to only 30 percent for Democratic members. For the two later periods, the comparable percentages were 37 versus 8 and 58 versus 46. These differences in voting patterns are sufficiently wide in the first two periods that the hypothesis that members of both parties vote in the same manner can be rejected at better than the 1 percent level; however, for the 1975–1983 period, the hypothesis can be rejected only at the 10 percent level.[23]

As the breakdown reveals, much more than political affiliation is involved in the decision process. In both the affirmative and negative determinations by the commission as a whole, the majority of the members of each party voted the same way. For example, under the 1974 trade law, 73 percent of the votes by Democratic commissioners and 94 percent of those by Republicans were affirmative in those cases where a majority found injury to exist. Similarly, for the negative determinations since 1974, the comparable percentages were 91 and 89, respectively. In fact, during the period 1949–1962, 58 percent of the decisions were unanimous. For the second and third periods, the figures were 56 percent and 40 percent, respectively. In the split decision cases during the first two periods, the voting pattern of Democratic commissioners was similar to that in the negative cases, whereas that of the Republican members resembled the pattern of the positive cases. In the period 1975–1983, this pattern was less evident.

One means of testing whether a president appoints members of the opposition party who share his party's attitudes toward trade policy is to compare their voting

records with the records of opposition party commissioners appointed by a president of their party. Between 1946
and mid-1983 presidents appointed or reappointed thirteen individuals whose political affiliation differed from
their own. An examination of the voting record of these
commissioners on import injury cases indicates that nine
of the thirteen individuals behaved much like the other
commissioners with the same party affiliation rather than
like members of the appointing president's party. Three of
the others followed a voting pattern more similar to members of the opposition party, and one adopted an intermediate voting position. In view of the well-known
differences in voting behavior that exist even among commissioners who share the president's political affiliation,
these figures seem to show that, in general, presidents do
not make a special effort to appoint members of the opposition party who share their own party's trade policy views.

Another method of avoiding the intention of the political
affiliation provision is to nominate independents who
share the administration's trade policy goals. Through
1982 this tactic had been followed only three times since
President Wilson first used it. Presidents John F. Kennedy,
Lyndon B. Johnson, and Jimmy Carter each appointed an
independent to what normally would have been a Republican position on the commission. The first appointee, Commissioner James Culliton, voted negatively along with his
five colleagues in all eleven escape clause cases in which he
participated. The second independent member, Commissioner Penelope Thunberg, whose term overlapped that of
Commissioner Culliton, voted in three cases (one of which
involved two parts) in which there was a divided opinion.
In these cases, 43 percent of the votes by Democratic commissioners were for a finding of injury, in contrast to 64
percent affirmative votes by the Republican members.
Commissioner Thunberg followed the voting pattern of

the Democratic members more closely than the Republican commissioners by finding injury in only one of the four decisions. Michael Calhoun, President Carter's appointee as an independent, participated in only two decisions where the vote was not unanimous. None of the votes cast by the Democratic commissioners in these cases was affirmative, whereas 75 percent of the votes by Republicans supported a positive injury determination. Calhoun's vote in both cases was, like the Democrats', negative. While these cases are hardly sufficient to reach a firm conclusion, they are consistent with the avoidance hypothesis. However, since the last two appointments are also consistent with the efforts of Presidents Johnson and Carter to increase the representation of women and minorities in the executive branch, they may not have been motivated at all by a desire to produce commission decisions more indicative of the trade policy views of the presidents' own political party.

The comparatively small number of commission appointments in which the party affiliation of the appointee differed from that of the president also may reflect either a deliberate effort by the White House to influence commission decisions or simply the greater difficulties in processing nominations from the opposition party. Between 1946 and mid-1983 there were forty-nine appointments and reappointments to the ITC. The appointees in thirty of these cases shared the party affiliation of the president at the time of their appointment, three were independents, and only sixteen were members of the opposition party. Conceivably this difference could be accounted for by a much longer average term of office of the latter groups, but the average length of opposition party appointments was actually somewhat shorter than same-party appointments.

In summary, the framers of the act establishing the ITC were correct in believing that party affiliation would signif-

icantly affect the voting pattern of commissioners; however, although Republican members still cast a higher
proportion of affirmative votes, party affiliation is no
longer as significant in explaining the voting pattern of the
commission as it was in the period from around 1950 to the
mid-1970s. The fact that party affiliation has an influence
suggests the hypothesis that when a vacancy on the commission for the opposition party occurs, presidents will
systematically try to select opposition party members who
share the trade policy views of the president's party. The
evidence does not seem to support this supposition. But
there is some weak support for the proposition that presidents have influenced the commission's voting pattern by
sometimes selecting independents rather than members of
the main opposition party. The main motivation for such
selections, however, may have been factors other than a
deliberate effort to obtain commission decisions more consistent with the administration's views. Similarly the evidence supporting the proposition that presidents delay
opposition party appointments may reflect the greater
difficulties of processing such nominations rather than a
conscious effort to establish a commission majority that
shares the president's party affiliation.

Professional Experience and Political Benefits

A second factor that presidents take into consideration in
screening prospective candidates for ITC positions is the
professional experience of the individuals. A basic requirement for any appointee is for the person to be able to carry
out the duties of the office in a manner that avoids the
politically damaging charge of incompetence. But there is
considerable room for disagreement among commissioners
because of the general nature of the guidelines established
by Congress for their decision making. Moreover, due to

the technical nature of the position, it is difficult to predict prior to a person's appointment how the individual will interpret the law. One basis used for judging the future behavior of candidates for commission appointments is their professional background and employment experience. Since presidents must assess issues in broad national and international terms, they are likely to favor individuals whose employment experience influences them to view trade policy matters in a similar manner rather than simply in sectoral terms. Persons who have worked for extensive periods in the executive branch or who are academics tend to possess this orientation.

As table 3.2 indicates, during the post–World War II period when the power of the president in trade policy matters was at its height, ITC appointments, not surprisingly, consisted mainly of individuals who had been employed in the executive branch and within the commission itself or who were academics. This pattern changed drastically after the late 1960s when Congress began to play a much more active role in determining the membership of the commission. Between 1968 and mid-1983, eight of the sixteen confirmed nominees had recent congressional experience either as staff personnel or as members of Congress (two persons). In the earlier period only one individual had congressional experience (as a member of

Table 3.2
Employment experience of ITC appointees, 1953–1983

	1953–1967	1968–1983
Academic	3	0
Executive branch	5	1
Congress	1	8
Private sector	2	7
Commission staff	2	0
Total	13	16

Congress). The proportion of commissioners from the private sector also rose significantly in the latter period. The tradition of appointing academics with economic or legal expertise in the trade field, as well as experts on the staff of the commission, was not followed at all during the period from 1968 to 1983.

Several factors account for the stronger role of Congress in the appointment process. Two closely related reasons are the significant increase in protectionist pressures from both workers and management in response to the rapid rise in import penetration ratios and the general belief that the trade adjustment provisions of the Trade Expansion Act of 1962 were ineffective. For example, a study made by the ITC during this period at the request of the Ways and Means Committee indicated sharp rises in the degree of import penetration in such sectors as textiles, footwear, automobiles, steel, and certain electrical consumer goods, including television sets, radios, and phonographs.[24] However, not a single affirmative decision under the new adjustment assistance program was made until November 1969. Thus as part of their response to the protectionist pressures from their constituents, members of Congress attempted much more vigorously than at any other time during the postwar period to ensure the selection of commissioners who would be more sympathetic to the competitive problems of U.S. industry. Like the president, they believed that appointees who had employment experience in the same branch of government as themselves were more likely to implement their trade policy goals than individuals with entirely different professional backgrounds.

In addition to these economic reasons, there was a specific issue that touched on the powers of Congress versus the president. It involved the antidumping code negotiated during the Kennedy Round as an agreement on the implementation of Article VI of the GATT and signed by the United States as an executive agreement. The Congress, and especially Senator Russell Long, chairman of the Senate Finance Committee, believed that the code should have been submitted to Congress for approval much in the same way the agreement on the American Selling Price (ASP) system had been. In particular, Congress objected to the statement in the code that a determination of injury would be made only when dumped imports were the principal cause of material injury to a domestic industry. The 1921 antidumping act had merely required a finding that dumping was causing injury to a domestic industry, and attorneys in the Office of the Special Trade Representative had regarded the code as consistent with the 1921 law. Therefore they did not believe the code required congressional approval. In 1969 Congress passed a law directing the ITC to ignore the new code in making its decisions on whether injury was occurring as a result of dumping.

In addition to pressing for congressional action on the matter, Senator Long and his committee colleagues began not only to quiz prospective commissioners on their attitudes toward the dumping controversy and the responsibilities of the commission generally but to oppose nominees who they felt would represent the attitudes of the executive branch in their decision making. This trend first became apparent in September 1967 when President Johnson nominated Stanley D. Metzger as a member and chairman of the ITC. Metzger was a professor at Georgetown Law School at the time but for several years had served as a legal adviser to the Department of State and also as a consultant to the Kennedy administration on the formulation of the Trade Expansion Act. Although the Senate Finance Committee and the Senate voted favorably on his nomination, Senator Long and especially Senator Vance Hartke subjected Professor Metzger to a period of intense questioning on the antidumping code, prompting a fellow committee member to state that he did not see why Senator Hartke was continuing "to castigate this witness with the line of questioning you are developing."[25]

When in April 1968 President Johnson nominated Bernard Norwood, a senior staff member of the Office of the Special Trade Representative and the person who had chaired the key interagency committee that made recommendations on trade issues, Senator Long and his committee colleagues withheld their approval on the grounds that approval would result in three members of the commission—Norwood, Metzger, and Thunberg—being ex-administration aides who had been involved in the Kennedy Round of trade negotiations.[26] Since they believed the president had usurped the functions of Congress on the matter of the antidumping code, these members of Congress were determined to press for more commissioners sympathetic to the viewpoint of Congress on the dumping as well as other trade matters.

A vacancy on the commission following the expiration of the term of James Culliton, one of the two independent members, provided an opportunity to resolve the impasse between the president and Congress. President Johnson selected Herschel Newsom, a Republican who had been president of the International Federation of Agricultural Producers and who had served on the Advisory Committee on Trade Negotiations under Presidents Kennedy and Johnson. According to Senator Long, the committee informed the White House that it would agree to Newsom only if one of the two nominees (the other then being Norwood) understood the problem with the antidumping issues: that an act of Congress cannot be repealed by an executive agreement. The administration suggested some alternatives to Norwood, and the committee did also. Finally in September 1968, the administration nominated Will E. Leonard, a former legislative assistant to Senator

Long and then a professional staff member of the Senate
Finance Committee. In his appearance before the committee, Leonard stated his view that the commission was a
fact-finding agency that was to act at the behest of Congress and, to a degree, at the behest of the president. He
declared that he would bring a lot of bias to the job, particularly the viewpoint of the Senate Finance Committee on
dumping issues.[27] After a statement by Senator Long to
Newsom, still a nominee, that he thought commission reports were sometimes slanted toward the executive
branch, both Leonard and Newsom were approved by the
committee and later by the Senate as a whole.

At regular intervals Senator Long and his committee colleagues continued to emphasize to prospective commissioners that "it is to the Congress, not the Executive, that
the Tariff Commission is expected to be responsive."[28] In
reacting to such admonitions, most nominees, including
Catherine Bedell in 1971[29] and William Alberger in 1977,[30]
asserted that they regarded the commission as a fact-
finding arm of Congress. More important than such statements is the fact that most appointees to the commission
since 1975 have had experience either as members of
Congress or as staff members of a key congressional
committee.

Whether this shift in the composition of the commission
has had any effect on the voting pattern of the group is not
clear. As table 3.1 indicates, since 1975 both Democratic
and Republican members of the ITC have been more protectionist in import injury cases (52 percent affirmative voting decisions) than they were in the period from 1949 to
1962 (40 percent affirmative voting decisions), even though
the safeguard rules are now roughly the same as they were
in that earlier period. However, both appointees with and
without congressional backgrounds have cast a higher

proportion of affirmative ballots than did their 1950 colleagues.

One difference that might be expected in the voting behavior of commissioners with and without a congressional background is that the former would have placed a greater emphasis on short-run factors in reaching their decisions. Members of Congress are continually subjected to short-run economic pressures and must be concerned about these pressures if they are to remain in office. Anticipating somewhat the analysis of the escape clause decisions of the commission and its individual members made in the next section, the two most significant variables influencing the decisions of individual members seem to have been the short-run change in an industry's profit rate and the long-run change in an industry's employment level. In the best-fit equation for the five commissioners in the sample— Daniel Minchew (Democrat), George Moore (Republican), Catherine Bedell (Republican), Joseph Parker (Republican), and Italo Ablondi (Democrat)—the logit estimate for the profit variable was higher than for the employment variable for Minchew and Bedell, the two appointees with congressional experience, and lower for Moore and Parker. For Ablondi, the profit variable also had a higher logit estimate than the employment variable. Thus there is some, though very weak, support for the hypothesis that those with a congressional background have a greater short-run sensitivity.

It might also have been expected that commissioners with a congressional background would be more receptive to those escape clause cases that either the Congress or the president had urged the ITC to investigate. In the probit analysis, a dummy variable measuring this effect was significant at the 10 percent or better level for Bedell and Parker and was nearly so for Moore though not for Minchew and Ablondi. Thus this hypothesis does not seem to be supported by the evidence.

In summary the recent history of the ITC appointment process provides another illustration of the efforts by Congress to recover some of the trade policy powers it had earlier delegated to the president. During the 1950s and most of the 1960s when the president's authority over trade matters was at its height, the president relied mainly on individuals with experience in the executive branch or on the commission itself for ITC appointees. In the late 1960s, however, Congress became dissatisfied with the president's behavior in the trade field on the grounds that it was not being brought into the decision-making process sufficiently and that the president was too liberal in his trade policy decisions. Consequently key congressional leaders, especially on the Senate Finance Committee, began to assert much greater control over the ITC appointment process and to insist that a significant share of the appointments go to individuals with staff or legislative experience in Congress. The impact of this shift in the composition of the commission is difficult to separate from that of the change Congress brought about in the trade laws, but the combination of the two produced a major change in the ITC's decision pattern in import injury cases. In the period 1963–1974 under the Trade Expansion Act of 1962, only 28 percent of the case decisions were affirmative or evenly split in contrast to 60 percent between 1975 and 1983 under the Trade Act of 1974. In the pre-1962 period, when the injury criteria were quite similar to the present ones, the affirmative and evenly split proportion was 41 percent. Either a larger fraction of the cases brought before the commission in the 1975–1983 period are more deserving of an affirmative injury determination or the ITC has become more protectionist.

In addition to considering the political affiliation and employment experience of ITC candidates, a president is likely to take into account the possible political debts he can repay or future political help he might obtain by appointing particular individuals. He can utilize the appointment opportunity for such diverse purposes as rewarding an individual for previous political service, building up support within a politically powerful economic sector, helping to gain the support of certain members of Congress for his other trade policies or for quite different programs, or improving his record of appointments of women, minorities, and representatives of certain religions, nationalities, geographic areas, and other groups.

A review of the appointments in the post–World War II period indicates surprisingly little behavior along the lines one would expect on the basis of the common interest or pressure group model of the political process. Out of the thirty-four individuals appointed one or more times between 1946 and mid-1983, only three were closely associated with particular manufacturing sectors and another three with agriculture.[31] Since the late 1960s, administrations have made greater efforts to nominate women and minorities, but the major factor influencing the selection process has been the pressure from Congress to appoint individuals with experience in the legislative branch of the federal government. Presidents have found that the benefits from yielding to this pressure have generally dominated other political considerations.

3.4 Decision Making in Import Relief Cases

Since ITC members are appointed rather than elected, the manner in which import policy pressures can affect their behavior differs considerably from the way these forces can influence members of Congress or the president. The preceding section analyzed how the commission's voting

behavior might be influenced by various political considerations brought to bear on the appointment process. This
section looks at whether political pressures, especially
from Congress and the president, influence the voting patterns of commissioners after they have been appointed. In
addition, the analysis is designed to determine how closely
the ITC follows the economic guidelines set forth in relevant trade legislation.

Political Pressures and Commission Behavior

Although political pressures could conceivably affect the
nature of a commissioner's decisions through their impact
on job satisfaction and future employment prospects, the
fact that the term of office extends for nine years and is not
renewable suggests that, once in office, a commissioner is
most likely, as Congress intended, to make decisions
based on a strict interpretation of the law. In the commission's semijudicial working environment, in which diver-
gent views on trade policy are frequently expressed,
striving for impartiality and technical competence tends to
be the best way to satisfy a person's desire for acceptance
and appreciation by fellow commissioners and staff, as
well as outside groups. Even commissioners who intend to
use the position as a stepping-stone to more influential or
better-paying positions within government or the private
sector will find that a reputation for impartiality and technical competence is helpful. In particular, as in the case of
elective offices, seeming to oppose the preferences of the
majority consistently (as they are manifest in this situation
by the trade laws governing commission behavior) is likely
to decrease a person's chances of obtaining other desirable
positions. Even pressure groups that may be favored by
biased decisions usually do not wish to employ an individual who will be dismissed by others as an unbalanced ad-

vocate. Consequently it appears most likely that any differences in the voting behavior of commissioners will tend to be based on differences in basic attitudes about the causes and effects of import competition that were developed prior to appointment.

Although individual commissioners are well insulated from political pressures, this may be less true for the commissioners collectively. Part of each member's job satisfaction will be determined by the reputation of the ITC as a whole within other parts of the federal government and the private sector. Moreover unlike the individual civil servant or even member of Congress, each commissioner is likely to see the group as small enough for an individual's decisions to count in determining this outside evaluation.

Under the present circumstances, in which Congress plays an active role in the appointment process, determines the budget, and reviews presidential decisions inconsistent with those of the commission, it might be expected that the agency would be particularly sensitive to congressional influences. For example, if the House Ways and Means Committee or the Senate Finance Committee passed by a large majority a resolution requesting an import relief investigation, it is clear that Congress and important private common interest groups would want a favorable decision from the commission. Not to reach such a finding if the case is plausible is to risk both bad publicity from Congress and direct punishment in the form of a rejection of requests for budget increases.

Pressures from the president are also likely to have an effect on ITC decisions. If, for example, the White House repeatedly rejects affirmative escape clause findings by the ITC, citing the same criteria the commissioners followed in reaching their decision, commission members are likely to begin to rethink their decision-making guidelines in the light of this obvious verdict of incompetence by the executive branch. While the White House is less likely than Congress to publicize its views nationally, their dissemination within the bureaucracy and in Washington could have a significant adverse impact on the level of job satisfaction of most commissioners.

Analysis of Import Relief Decisions
under the Trade Act of 1974

The Trade Act of 1974 significantly changed the criteria for determining serious injury (or threat of serious injury) from those set forth in the Trade Expansion Act of 1962. The earlier act specified that an affirmative determination required injury to have been the result "in major part" of concessions granted under trade agreements and increased imports to have been "the major factor" in causing this injury. For several years after the act was passed, the commission adopted a strict interpretation of these provisions and unanimously rejected all cases brought before it. Some commissioners eventually adopted a less rigid interpretation of these terms, and an affirmative decision was finally made in 1969. Nevertheless the ITC remained divided, and only two affirmative decisions were made during the entire period in which this law applied.[32]

The 1974 act eliminated the need for any connection between increased imports and previous tariff concessions.[33] In addition the increased imports only had to be "a substantial cause" of serious injury, with "substantial cause" defined as a "cause which is important and not less than any other cause."[34]

In determining whether "an article is being imported into the United States in such increased quantities as to be a substantial cause of serious injury," the commission was directed to take into account all economic factors it considered relevant, including (but not limited to) "the significant idling of productive facilities in an industry, the inability of a significant number of firms to operate at a reasonable level of profit, and significant unemployment or underemployment within the industry."[35] With respect to the threat of serious injury, the factors suggested by the framers of the act as relevant were "a decline in sales, a higher and growing inventory, and a downward trend in production, profits, wages, or employment (or increasing underemployment) in the domestic industry."[36] With respect to substantial cause, the suggested factors were "an increase in imports (either actual or relative to domestic production) and a decline in the proportion of the domestic market supplied by domestic producers."[37]

The reports issued by the ITC on import relief cases under the Trade Act of 1974 have included a more extensive and consistent set of economic data relating to the industry than did its reports under previous laws. In addition to information on imports, exports, and production over a five-year period, the new series of reports includes data over this time period on the ratio of profits to sales, employment levels, inventory changes, source of imports, location of domestic firms, and changes in the number of these firms. In some cases data covering productivity, capital utilization, technological change, and wages are also presented, but in most instances these are not sufficiently extensive to be included in a formal statistical analysis.

Table 3.3 presents the various combinations of the variables that best explain the proportion of commissioners declaring that serious injury had occurred in the import injury cases investigated between 1974 and 1983. The two variables that almost always turned up as significant (either alone or together) in the many combinations of variables tested are a change in the percentage rate of net profits to sales over the last two comparable six-month periods (or, if not given, the last two years) and the aver-

Table 3.3
Factors influencing serious injury determinations of the ITC

Equation	CON	DPSR	DELR	NPE	MC	CX	Adj. R^2	F statistic
1	58.30	−1.97	−1.02				0.12	4.38**
	(9.47)***	(−2.36)**	(−2.31)**					
2	47.9	−1.36	−.73	34.1			.26	6.53***
	(7.23)***	(−1.71)*	(−1.75)*	(3.03)***				
3	48.75	−1.80	−.98		.30		.13	3.32**
	(4.53)***	(−2.11)**	(−2.21)**		(1.08)			
4	34.54	−1.09	−.66	36.24	.40		.29	5.68***
	(3.23)***	(−1.35)	(−1.58)	(3.25)***	(1.57)			
5	33.57	−.98	−.58	37.80	.39	8.48	.28	4.51***
	(3.07)***	(−1.17)	(−1.29)	(3.24)***	(1.51)	(.50)		

Note: Dependent variable = percentage of commissioners voting who found injury; CON = constant term; DPSR = change in percentage rate of net profits to sales over the most recent two comparable time periods of six months or two years; DELR = average annual percentage change in employment over the last five years; NPE = 1,0 dummy variable indicating whether DPSR and DELR are both negative (1) or not (0); MC = average ratio of imports to consumption over the last five years; CX = 1,0 dummy variable indicating whether the investigation was requested by either the Congress or the president (1) or not (0). Number of observations = 47.

*Significant at the 10 percent level for t-values of the regression coefficients or the F statistic.
**Significant at the 5 percent level for t-values of the regression coefficients or the F statistic.
***Significant at the 1 percent level for t-values of the regression coefficients or the F statistic.

age annual percentage change in employment over the last five years. Moreover introducing a dummy variable to capture the possibility of a nonlinear relationship when these were both negative further improved the equations' fit. If an industry's profit rate dropped 3 percentage points between the last two years and employment also had declined on an average of 3 percent annually over the last five years, the regression results (equation 2) indicate that these factors would have been responsible for about 40 percent of the commissioners' voting affirmatively on serious injury.

Variations in the forms of the profit and employment variables, such as the average change in the profit rate over the last five years, the average level of net profits to sales, and the percentage change in employment over the last year, are either not significant or perform considerably more poorly than the other three variables. A fourth economic variable that sometimes comes close to being significant at the 10 percent level in the expected direction is the average ratio of imports to consumption over the last five-year period.[38] Rather surprisingly neither the short-run nor the long-run change in the import penetration ratio is significant. Among the other economic variables tried in the regression analysis were short-run and long-run percentage changes in industry shipments, imports, and productivity, as well as short-run percentage changes in consumption, inventories, and the ratio of inventories to sales. These variables either were not significant or did not perform nearly as well as the profit and employment variables.

In summary, three economic variables turn out to be statistically significant: the change in the percentage rate of net profits to sales over the last two comparable six-month periods (or, if not given, the last two years), the average annual percentage change in employment over the last five years, and a dummy variable to capture the possibility of a nonlinear relationship when the first two variables are both negative. This last relationship is especially strong. Over one-third of the commissioners tend to vote affirmatively on serious injury if there is a short-run drop in profits coupled with a longer-run decline in employment.

Equation 5 includes a variable indicating whether the president or the Congress requested the import relief investigation. The sign is as expected, but the coefficient is not significant. Other political variables also are not significantly related to commission decisions. These included the proportion of commissioners voting who were either Democrats or Republicans, the size of an industry as measured either by total employment or value of output, and whether labor groups joined management in requesting an investigation. Neither is there a protectionist bias against imports from developing countries or Japan. A dummy variable constructed to reflect whether the industry applying for import relief was concentrated in one or two states or was widely dispersed also did not provide any explanatory power for commission decisions. Finally, in order to determine whether commissioners were more sympathetic to import competition problems of industries that were important in the areas where they had spent a significant part of their professional careers, the decision making of individual commissioners was related to an industry location variable, as well as to the various other factors previously discussed.[39] No decision-making relation was found between an industry's location and the regional background of any commissioner.

There is a surprising degree of uniformity in the set of variables giving the best fit for each commissioner, with the short-run change in profits, the long-run change in employment, a dummy variable indicating whether these two variables are negative, and the level of the import penetration ratio usually giving the best results for each individual, just as these variables also did for the commission as a whole. There also did not seem to be any greater tendency for commissioners with congressional experience to respond in a protectionist manner in cases referred to the commission by Congress or the president than for those without this background.

Other investigators have also discovered certain common economic characteristics in the industries declared to be suffering injury. In an analysis of escape clause cases between 1948 and 1954, Kravis found that a decline in production and low profits were used as the main test of serious injury.[40] Similarly for the period 1951–1962, Peterson determined that domestic shipments and employment had declined in most of the industries judged to be seriously injured and that, with few exceptions, were less profitable than the average manufacturing industry.[41] Peterson did not compare the industries judged to be injured with those where no serious injury was found with respect to these variables.

A more recent study by Pearson did make such a comparison for recent import injuries.[42] After comparing "injured" and "noninjured" industries (as judged by the commission) with respect to such variables as the average ratio of profits to sales, trends in employment, and average capacity utilization, Pearson concluded that "the indices of injury were not as expected. If anything, injury appears more prevalent in the negative determinations than the positive ones."[43]

In summary, it appears that the aim of the founders of the ITC to free the decisions of the agency from the influence of current political pressures has been achieved by and large. In making their decisions in import relief cases, the commissioners do not seem to be swayed by the views of Congress and the president on particular cases or by the ability of private interest groups to exert political power. Instead they tend to be mainly influenced by three economic conditions in the industry under consideration: the short-run change in its profits, the longer-term shift in its employment level, and, in particular, whether both of these two variables are negative.

3.5 Summary

This chapter began with a review of the functions of the ITC and how they have changed since its formation in 1916. Then drawing on the different models of trade policy behavior, various factors (including those required by law) likely to influence the president and the Congress in appointing members to the commission were discussed, and evidence concerning whether they affected the nature of ITC appointments was examined.

One such matter analyzed was the effect on commission decisions of the requirement that no more than three of the commissioners be members of the same political party. Throughout the period 1949–1983, Republican members cast a significantly higher proportion of affirmative votes than Democrats; however, the significance of party affiliation has weakened considerably since around 1975. Both Republicans and Democrats cast a higher proportion of affirmative votes in the 1975–1983 period than in either the 1963–1974 or 1949–1962 periods. No strong evidence supports the hypothesis that a president seeks to nominate only members of the opposite party who share the views of his own party. Furthermore, the size of the sample is too small to conclude that presidents tend to pick independent commissioners rather than those of the opposition party in order to influence the pattern of decisions. While presidents tended to delay appointing opposition party members longer than members of their own party, this may simply reflect the greater difficulty of obtaining agreement within their administration and Congress on whom to nominate rather than indicate a deliberate effort to shape the pattern of ITC decisions.

An important finding in the section on the appointment process concerns the extent to which the Congress has influenced the nature of ITC appointments in recent years. By failing to confirm routinely presidential nominees to the commission, the Senate has forced recent presidents to nominate more individuals who have had employment experience in Congress and the private sector rather than in the executive branch or academe.

One reason for this increased congressional intervention has been to ensure the selection of individuals who agree that the ITC should be more responsive to Congress than to the president on questions involving the authority of these two branches of government over trade policy. Some members of Congress also supported this position because they thought it would lead to the selection of commissioners who would reflect the more protectionist views of Congress as compared to those of the president; however, the shift in the background of the commissioners does not appear to have had any major effect on the voting pattern of the commissioners.

The chapter concludes by analyzing the decisions of the ITC under section 201 of the 1974 Trade Act (the so-called escape clause provision) from two viewpoints. The first is whether the commission has followed a consistent and measurable set of economic standards in deciding whether a petitioning industry should be given import relief. The second is whether political pressures from the Congress, the president, or the private sector have influenced these decisions. Regression analysis indicates significant economic differences between industries that are recommended for import relief and those that are not. In affirmative cases the industries are characterized by a recent decline in profits and a longer-run drop in employment. Various political factors such as whether the president or Congress requests the investigation, the size of the industry, or whether labor joins management in requesting an investigation are not significantly related to whether the decisions are affirmative or negative.

4   Decision Making at the Presidential Level

Although Congress has exercised its constitutional power to regulate international trade much more fully in recent years, the president's authority to shape import policy is still enormous.[1] The first section of this chapter briefly describes this authority and how it has changed since the 1930s, while the other five sections analyze the political and economic factors that have influenced import decisions by the executive branch. More specifically, section 4.2 discusses in general terms the types of political pressures brought on the president and his representatives and their likely reactions to these influences. Some of the hypotheses developed in this section are then tested in section 4.3 by examining presidential decisions on import injury cases in which the ITC has recommended some form of import assistance. The following section describes the circumstances leading to the introduction of the trigger price system for steel imports in order to illustrate the complex manner in which private industry, the Congress, and the president interact in the formation of trade policy. In section 4.5 the various models set forth in chapter 1 dealing with the behavior of government officials on the issue of protection versus trade liberalization are tested by utilizing data on the interindustry variations in the depth of duty cuts offered in the Tokyo and Kennedy rounds of multilateral trade negotiations. The models are also tested against pre-Tokyo Round tariff levels across industries and the incidence of nontariff trade barriers in these sectors. The last section summarizes the results of the various analyses.

4.1 Presidential Powers to Control Imports

The extent of the president's tariff-reducing authority has varied in an almost cyclical manner. Periods in which the executive branch has been given significant tariff-cutting authority by the Congress—1934–1939, 1945–1948, 1962–1967, and 1974–1979—have usually been followed by periods of very little or no duty-reducing authority. There has also been considerable variation in the degree to which Congress has restrained the president in the use of duty-cutting authority already granted him. For example, in the 1948 law extending the trade agreements program, Congress included a so-called peril point clause that prevented the president from entering into a trade agreement until the ITC had determined the limits of the duty cuts that could be made without causing or threatening to cause injury to domestic industries producing articles similar to those being considered for duty reductions.[2] This provision was repealed in 1949, reintroduced in 1951, and eliminated in the 1962 Trade Act. Under this last law the commission was merely directed to make a judgment "as to the probable economic effect of modification of duties."[3] This provision was retained in the 1974 Trade Act, but the president was required to establish a system for obtaining advice from the private sector, a change that has somewhat reduced the degree of the president's independence to select items on which duty cuts are to be made and to determine the depth of those cuts. Requiring and then strengthening congressional representation at all trade negotiations under the 1962 and 1974 acts has had the same effect. Since 1954 the president has also been directed not to decrease duties on any article if he finds that doing so threatens to impair national security.

In addition to the various changes in the restrictions on the president's duty-cutting powers, since the 1950s there has been a trend toward reducing the ability of the president to turn aside recommended or requested increases in protection for an industry. The provision introduced in the 1958 Trade Act and strengthened in the 1962 and 1974 trade laws that permitted Congress to override a presidential rejection of an affirmative ITC import injury finding is a good example. However, in 1983 the Supreme Court declared all such congressional veto provisions unconstitutional, and the Trade and Tariff Act of 1984 changed this provision to conform with the Supreme Court ruling. A weakening of presidential authority has occurred in the areas of dumping, subsidization, and unfair trade practices. Until 1954 the secretary of the treasury determined both whether dumping had occurred and whether it had caused injury. The latter function was transferred to the ITC in that year. Under the Trade Agreements Act of 1979, the determination of injury in subsidy cases was also made a responsibility of the commission. In both instances Congress viewed the assignment of these functions to the commission as offsetting a tendency of the executive branch to be too liberal in its policy-implementing role. The imposition in 1974 of shorter time limits for decisions by the Treasury in subsidy and dumping cases was another manifestation of Congress's dissatisfaction with the performance of the executive branch. In response to a provision inserted by Congress in the Trade Agreements Act of 1979, the president shifted the administration of the antidumping and countervailing duty laws from the Treasury to the

Commerce Department in 1979. Most members of Congress believed that Commerce would follow the intent of Congress more closely than the Treasury Department had.

The manner in which the law on unfair import practices (section 337 of the Tariff Act of 1930) has changed further illustrates how presidential powers have been weakened because Congress felt most presidents were too lenient in administering the law. Under the 1922 and 1930 acts, the president had been given the power to exclude articles from entry into the United States if unfair methods of import competition (mostly patent infringements) were being practiced. The ITC assisted the president by undertaking the investigations and making recommendations, but the decision of the president was conclusive. The 1974 trade bill gave the commission itself the authority to exclude imports of affected articles or to issue cease-and-desist orders with regard to such practices. The president's role was reduced to being able to overturn these decisions within a sixty-day period "for policy reasons."

At the same time that Congress was diluting the president's power to reduce trade barriers and to prevent ITC recommendations for import-restricting actions from being implemented, it was giving him new authority to limit imports. The 1922 and 1930 tariff acts had granted the president the authority to impose new or additional duties on imports or even to exclude imports from countries that had imposed unreasonable regulations on U.S. products or discriminated against U.S. commerce. The 1962 trade act further directed the president to take all appropriate and feasible steps to eliminate "unjustifiable" foreign import restrictions (including the imposition of duties and other import restrictions). In addition, he could suspend or withdraw previously granted concessions if other countries impose trade restrictions that "substantially burden" U.S. commerce, engage in discriminating acts, or maintain unreasonable import restrictions.[4] The Trade Act of 1974 restated and expanded somewhat these provisions,[5] and the 1979 act stressed the president's responsibility for enforcing U.S. rights under any trade agreement and simplified the list of foreign practices against which he was directed to take action.[6] The 1984 act expanded the president's retaliatory authority to include restrictions on the provision of services by foreigners and defined in more detail the terms *unreasonable, unjustifiable,* and *discriminatory.*

In 1955 Congress granted the president the right to adjust the level of imports of any article if he found it was being imported in such quantities "as to threaten to impair the national security."[7] The list of broad criteria for taking such an action that Congress added in 1958 has made it possible for the president to impose quantitative import restrictions in almost any major sector for national security reasons. Initially the Office of Defense Mobilization or the Office of Emergency Planning was directed to investigate requests for protection on national security grounds, but under the 1974 Trade Act, this function was transferred to the Treasury. The 1979 reorganization of foreign trade activities then transferred this responsibility to the Commerce Department. Although there have been a number of industry petitions over the years for import relief on national security grounds (section 232 of the Trade Expansion Act of 1962), the president has granted protection only in the case of crude and refined petroleum.

Changes in the manner in which the president can treat an affirmative import relief finding by the ITC is another example of the increase in the presidential power to restrict trade. During the 1950s the president was limited to either accepting the import relief recommendations of the commission or not granting any form of relief. Under the 1962 and 1974 trade acts, however, the president was given the authority to introduce the import restrictions he believed most appropriate. In particular, the President was given—and still has—the authority to negotiate orderly marketing agreements with foreign countries limiting exports from these countries after he receives an affirmative ITC decision.

As with ITC decisions, determinations by the president and his administrative agencies can be appealed through the courts. For example, negative determinations by the secretary of commerce concerning the existence of dumping or foreign subsidies can be appealed to the Court of International Trade, as can matters relating to the proper appraised value or duty rate for imports in import relief and section 22 actions by the president.[8] Similarly determinations by the secretary of labor on adjustment assistance petitions by workers can be reviewed by the Court of International Trade.[9] The final decision in all such cases is vested in the U.S. Supreme Court, if it wishes to accept an appeal from a lower court.

4.2 Import Policy Behavior at the Executive Branch Level

The president is the only U.S. official (other than the vice-president) who is elected from a political marketplace in which all the national implications of a public policy are internalized. One important implication is that voters hold the president more responsible than other elected officials (members of Congress or governors) for policy goals with significant national effects. For example, while members of Congress will be judged in part by their efforts to stem inflation, it is the president for whom inflation will be a major political issue. On the other hand, members of Congress are more likely than the president to be held accountable for a failure to obtain a national park in their districts or to secure assistance for a local industry faced with economic difficulties. Consequently in their efforts to be reelected and to increase their influence while in office, presidents will stress their ability to promote desirable national goals.

One desirable national goal voters expect a president to work for, especially because of the president's constitutional responsibilities in the foreign policy field, is a state of relationships with other countries that leads to general economic prosperity and international political stability. The president can follow a number of alternative policy approaches in order to be regarded by voters as performing well in the foreign policy area. Whether a president chooses to make trade issues a key part of his foreign policy agenda depends in part on the particular international problems of the time and his own public policy preferences.[10] Presidents Kennedy and Roosevelt—the latter through his secretary of state, Cordell Hull—did make trade policy a priority item on their policy agenda, whereas more recent presidents have considered trade policy to be of lesser importance in their policy programs. The success of Presidents Roosevelt, Kennedy, and Nixon in obtaining the authority from Congress to reduce tariffs significantly demonstrates the ability of a president to achieve particular goals if he is willing to use fully the enormous powers he has.

Regardless of whether they emphasize trade issues, presidents are likely to promote general trade liberalization rather than general protectionism. In dealing extensively with representatives of foreign countries, the president becomes more familiar and thus usually more sympathetic with their side of the story than does the typical member of Congress. More important, the public tends to hold the president responsible for the country's international economic image. In this regard the United States is viewed by other major industrial nations as the key participant in the liberal international order that developed after World War II. Furthermore these countries still basically support this regime and believe that if the United States were to introduce general protectionism, it would rapidly spread throughout the trading world. It is also a widely accepted view by officials in these countries, as well as by export and foreign investment interests in the United States, that such a shift in policy would not only lead to a collapse of the existing trade and financial order but would result in extensive job and financial losses in all countries. The apparent ability of foreign countries and domestic export and financial interests to persuade U.S. voters that this scenario is plausible means that a president runs considerable political risks if he openly pursues a policy of widespread protectionism.

At the same time it is very difficult for a president to resist granting protection to particular industries that are politically significant in voting and/or financial terms and that also seem to have a reasonably good case in terms of U.S. laws and GATT rules covering import relief and fair trade practices. Major industries such as textiles and apparel, steel, and automobiles possess the necessary resources to shift to the political track for gaining protection if the petitions for protection by way of more administrative or technical tracks, such as the import relief and fair trade provisions in U.S. trade law, are turned down.[11] In using the political route to protection, an industry will attempt to convince enough members of Congress concerning the validity of their case so that such steps are taken as congressional hearings that publicize the industry's plight and the introduction of legislation that directly provides protection. Furthermore the industry will spend large sums to publicize its case for assistance through various news and communication channels. The employees of the industry will also apply political pressure on members of

Congress through letters, visits, campaign contributions, and so forth. If these efforts by an industry are successful, the president will become convinced that the threat of members of Congress to enact protectionist legislation or block other desired legislation is creditable. Furthermore support for protecting the industry on such grounds as fairness, national defense, or the importance of a way of life will become widespread among the general public. In this situation the president is likely to agree to some protection for the industry because he fears that Congress will pass legislation that restricts imports to an even greater degree. The president also need not be too concerned about his image as a person who is implementing meritorious national goals, since the industry will have convinced the public that he is properly reacting against unfair foreign competition. Governments of foreign suppliers will be dissatisfied, but even this reaction can be minimized by negotiating orderly market agreements or pressing for voluntary export restraints only with those countries from which most of the increased imports come.

Small industries usually do not possess the necessary resources to utilize the political route to protection even if they are well organized. Consequently utilizing the reasoning based on the pressure group and voting machine models of political behavior, one would expect protection petitions by small industries generally to be rejected when a presidential decision is required, such as affirmative ITC cases under the import injury provisions (section 201 of the Trade Act of 1974) of U.S. trade law.

It was argued in chapter 1, however, that the pressure group and voting machine models must be modified to include the behavior of public officials based on various social concerns. For example, a president may concur in an affirmative ITC import injury case for a small industry because of his personal concern (or his perception of the

general public's concern) for adjustment or equity problems in the industry. The analysis in section 4.5 of the duty
cuts across industries in the Tokyo and Kennedy rounds of
trade negotiations will provide an opportunity to test the
relative importance of the short-run, self-interest models of
government behavior versus those models that take into
account social concerns or long-run self-interest.

The extent to which presidential actions are based on the
motivations underlying the short-run, self-interest models
versus the models emphasizing long-run self-interest or
social concerns also varies over time. For example, one
would expect the president to be more sympathetic to protection petitions the closer the time he must make a decision is to a national election and the lower his public rating
at the time. The consistency of a trade policy decision with
other national goals that the president is pursuing is also
relevant. If there is considerable inflation in the economy
and he has made the reduction of inflation a high priority
on the public policy agenda, the president is less likely to
grant protection to a particular industry lest he be accused
of undermining his inflation goal. On the other hand, he is
likely to be more receptive to protectionist action if unemployment is a significant national problem. A president's
effectiveness in dealing with Congress and the extent to
which his own party controls Congress are among other
factors influencing his actions.

Many trade policies are determined not by the president
or his political appointees but by civil servants who do not
derive their authority directly from the voters. Consequently an understanding of how trade policy is made also
requires an analysis of their likely behavior. In analyzing
the behavior of elected officials, it has been postulated that
the election process constrains these officials from simply
following their own public policy preferences. Instead they
must try to represent the wishes of the electorate suffi-

ciently to be reelected. Using this framework, the analysis here has focused on factors that determine the nature and intensity of voter preferences, why and how some voters form organizations to exert collective pressure on elected officials, and the nature of the policy preferences held by these officials.

Explaining the behavior of nonelected civil servants is in some ways more difficult. As with elected officials, nonelected officials are constrained by the policy preferences of others, but the ways in which these restrict their actions are much less direct and obvious. One way of getting at the manner in which these constraints operate is to start with the obvious point that the utility level of civil servants dealing with trade policy is usually affected much more by possible changes in their earnings and working conditions than by the direct consumption and indirect collective effects of any policy decisions they make. Therefore the main basis for their actions will be the effects on their career prospects. The question thus becomes, What determines the nature of these effects?

A typical government agency such as the Department of Commerce or Department of Labor is directed by the statute establishing it and by the subsequent duties assigned it to promote and control the interests of particular economic or social groups. In selecting the political appointees of the agency, from the secretary down at least to the assistant secretary level, the president usually tries to pick individuals supported by, or at least acceptable to, most common interest organizations representing these groups. Thus these pressure groups often have almost a veto power over the top political appointments. They also play a major role subsequently in shaping private and public opinion about whether the agency is doing a good job.

Since the top political appointees are generally already sympathetic to the economic problems of the groups they deal with and also want to be well regarded, both during their tenure in office and after they return to private life (often in the sector the agency represents), they quite naturally will try to promote the interests of their constituencies with the White House and other government agencies. Moreover these political appointees will judge the performance of the civil servants under them on the basis of how effective they are in carrying out the same objective.

This favorable attitude of government agencies toward the groups they deal with is regularly reinforced by personal contacts with representatives from these groups, which take place not only at the top political levels but throughout most of the bureaucracy. For example, officials in the Departments of Labor and Commerce who collect labor or business statistics or administer some regulation are frequently in touch with labor representatives and business executives, respectively. Similarly State and Agricultural Department employees, both in Washington and in the field, deal extensively with representatives of foreign governments and domestic farmers, respectively. Sometimes these official contacts relate to some specific economic difficulty, but even when they do not, discussions of economic problems often take place as part of the social conversation connected with any meeting. The same is true at the various professional conferences attended by senior bureaucrats and leaders from the economic community they assist.

Numerous officials in each government agency thus gain detailed on-the-job knowledge about the economic problems of those whose interests they address; however, they learn little about the difficulties faced by other groups, relying for this on their poorer off-the-job sources of information. This situation reinforces the tendency of these officials, as well as their entire agencies, to be sympathetic to the groups they represent. Still another reason why this favorable attitude develops and is strengthened is the important role that these groups play in meeting officials' desires for social acceptance and approbation. If officials openly express sympathy for the problems articulated by such groups, they are not only more likely to be accepted and praised but to obtain the kind of cooperation that enables them to perform their jobs more effectively.

As Stigler (1975) and Peltzman (1976) have argued, the net effect of these various factors is that civil servants at all levels in various government agencies tend to adopt the economic and social viewpoints of the groups they serve. In interagency meetings on trade matters, for example, officials from Agriculture will tend to promote the interests of domestic farmers, those from Labor and Commerce the viewpoint of U.S. labor unions and businesses, respectively, and representatives from State press the concerns of foreign governments. By behaving in this manner, they further their career objectives and improve their personal and professional relationships with those with whom they spend a significant part of their working lives. Niskanen (1971) argues that the personal objectives of bureaucrats will also lead them to try to maximize the size of their budgets. Sometimes the various influences on decision making that stem from the desire to be successful in the job are weak, and therefore nonelected officials have some latitude to follow their own policy preferences. These are most likely to occur when the decisions are being made by civil servants quite far removed from the political appointees or by political appointees whose other responsibilities tend to dwarf those on trade issues.

As is the case with elected and politically appointed officials, the educational and employment background of civil servants plays an important role in shaping their personal public policy preferences. A large proportion of nonelected individuals in relatively high-level government positions have moved directly into the government after completing their undergraduate or graduate education. With this background they tend to adopt a national viewpoint rather than one that favors particular common interest groups.

The tendency of government officials (like the typical consumer-voter) to be concerned about the economic conditions of that part of the population with whom they are most familiar underscores the importance of lobbying within the executive branch. As with congressional lobbying, the purpose is not only to remind government officials of the policy preferences of their constituencies but to personalize the economic difficulties these groups face. This latter objective is likely to prove more effective in influencing the decisions of civil servants than of elected officials, since nonelected officials are likely to have somewhat greater scope for following their own sympathies. However, even after officials within an agency become convinced that part of the community they represent has a good case for government assistance on national interest grounds, they must still compete for support within their own agency and in interagency committees against other claimants for special government help. If the case is not one where the political clout of the pressure group is obvious to all, decisions among competing claims tend to be determined by technically qualified senior civil servants on the basis of the soundness of the case. In the trade field, this means that careful analysis of both the relevant economic statistics and the legal implications of the situation is important in trying to obtain a favorable decision. Common interest groups who possess the resources necessary to touch base frequently with political appointees and senior civil servants in relevant agencies and to provide them with substantive analysis of their problems are likely to be more successful in obtaining help. Since the major constraint on possessing these capabilities is financial, there is likely to be a positive relationship between a pressure group's success at the interagency level and the magnitude of the financial resources it commits for lobbying at this level.

4.3 Presidential Actions on ITC Import Relief Cases

Prior to 1974 there was no mention in the law of any set of criteria the president should follow in deciding whether to accept or reject an affirmative import relief finding by the ITC. The 1951 and 1962 trade acts merely stated that the president "may" implement the recommendations of the commission. Presumably in granting the president this authority, Congress intended for the final decision to include consideration of the foreign policy implications of withdrawing tariff concessions, as well as of the impact of the increased imports on the competing domestic industry. However, the 1974 Trade Act stated that the president "shall provide import relief . . . , unless he determines that provision of such relief is not in the national economic interest of the United States."[12] Furthermore the president was directed to take into account several criteria in determining whether to grant import relief: the effect of import relief on the price to consumers of the imported article and its domestic substitute; the effect of import relief on the international economic interests of the United States; the impact on other U.S. industries as a result of any compensation or retaliation; the probable effectiveness of import relief as a means of promoting adjustment; and the economic and social costs incurred by taxpayers, communities, and workers in the event relief was not granted.

In addition to these economic criteria, certain other political factors are likely to be important in shaping the president's actions on ITC cases. For example, as hypothesized in the adding machine model, the president is more likely to act favorably if the injured industry is large in terms of employment. Cases in which labor is a petitioner or in which the Senate Finance Committee or House Ways and Means Committee recommends the investigation should have a higher than average chance of presidential approval. Furthermore the president is likely to be more receptive to import relief if his decision on a case must be made just before a presidential or congressional election. Still another likely period of high presidential vulnerability to protectionist pressures is when he is in the concluding stages of a multilateral trade negotiation. Finally, the president is not likely to grant relief if that action appears to run counter to a major policy goal he is actively pursuing.

Table 4.1 gives the results of testing these hypotheses by analyzing presidential import relief decisions (the dependent variable) from 1975 to 1979. Decisions in which the president granted import relief, either by accepting the substance of an ITC recommendation, by negotiating an orderly marketing agreement, or by taking some other restrictive action, were coded 1 in the logit analysis, while decisions rejecting import relief were coded 0. Various independent dummy variables were coded in the same manner. If an ITC decision or the initiation of an investigation occurred within August, September, or October 1974, 1976, or 1978 (periods just before an election), the case was coded 1, and if it occurred outside of these time periods, it was coded 0. It is expected that the coefficient between these variables and the dependent variable would be positive. Cases in which labor was or was not a petitioner for the investigation were coded 1 and 0, respectively, as were those in which either the Ways and Means or Senate Finance committees did (1) or did not (0) request the investigation. A positive relationship between these two independent variables and the dependent variable is expected,

Table 4.1
Factors influencing presidential decisions on affirmative ITC import relief cases, 1975–1979

Equation	ITC	INFL	DUNAV3	D1	D2	D3	Likelihood ratio statistic
1	6.5 (1.65)	−1.1 (−1.80)*		5.6 (1.70)			(10.1)**
2	6.4 (1.67)	−1.0 (−1.79)*				4.9 (1.61)	(7.9)*
3			2.4 (1.77)*		2.2 (1.72)*		(6.7)*
4		−0.3 (−2.24)**		3.3 (1.80)*	3.0 (2.09)*		(10.8)**

Note: Dependent variable = whether the president granted import relief (1) or did not (0). ITC = percentage of commissioners favoring import relief; INFL = annual inflation rate (GNP deflator) in the quarter preceding the ITC decision; DUNAV3 = difference between the average unemployment rate in the three quarters preceding the president's decision and in the three quarters prior to this period; D1 = whether the presidential decision was after (1) or before (0) July 1978; D2 = whether initiation of the ITC investigation was in August, September, or October in the years 1974, 1976, or 1978 (1) or not (0); D3 = whether the ITC decision was within these election periods (1) or not (0).

* t statistic significant at the 10 percent level.
** t statistic significant at the 5 percent level.

as is a positive correlation between the dependent variable and whether the president's decision occurred after the multilateral trade negotiations "statement of understanding" in July 1978 (coded 1) or before that date (coded 0).

The continuous variables used to explain presidential decisions are the percentage of the ITC voting members who reached a positive injury finding and various measures of inflation and unemployment rates (or changes in these rates) near the time of the president's or the ITC's decision. It is hypothesized that the higher the percentage of commissioners voting in the affirmative, the more likely is the president to accept their injury finding and to conclude that the economic and social costs to workers would be high if relief is not granted. Thus the relationship between the ITC variable and the dependent variable should be positive. The same is true with respect to the recent rate of unemployment. On the other hand, a negative correlation between the dependent variable and the recent inflation rate is likely.

As equations 1 and 2 in table 4.1 indicate, the ITC variable is not quite significant at the 10 percent level when introduced together with the rate of inflation and either the stage of the multilateral trade negotiations or the nearness of the ITC decision to a presidential or congressional election.[13] However, the inflation rate or change in this rate (not shown) always turns out to be significant in the various regressions tried with two or three variables. The unemployment variable (not shown) invariably appears with the wrong sign and occasionally is even significant. The change in unemployment is significant in the expected direction. The level of industry employment (not shown) is never significant, nor are the dummy variables indicating whether Congress requested the investigation or whether labor was a petitioner. However, the dummy variables indicating whether the president's decision occurs near the time of an election or during the concluding stages of the Tokyo Round negotiations are significant.

It thus appears that political factors influence presidential decisions in ITC cases; however, rather than being influenced by the voting strength of the injured industry, the president seems more concerned with creating the impression of being generally sympathetic to industry's import problems during periods when he or his congressional colleagues are running for office or when he wishes to gain congressional acceptance of a particular piece of trade legislation. It is also somewhat surprising that the president in this period apparently saw a closer relationship between anti-inflation programs and ITC decisions than between full employment efforts and these decisions. Furthermore, an unexpected result that raises questions about the entire ITC import relief process is the lack of a strong positive correlation between the degree of agreement among the commissioners and president's acceptance of the commission's recommendation.

4.4 Implementation of the Trigger Price Mechanism for the Steel Industry

Because of the national nature of his electoral constituency, a president must be highly sensitive to the effect that granting import protection to any particular industry in the economy has on his image as a leader who promotes the national interest. If the general public perceives the president's action as unfairly favoring that sector, he risks the loss of many more voters than he gains. Consequently a president is not likely to provide industry-specific protection unless he is convinced that those outside the assisted industry will support it on, for example, status quo grounds or as a form of insurance they may need someday.

The events leading to the introduction of the so-called

trigger price system to deal with the import problem faced by the steel industry in 1977 provide an excellent illustration of how an industry that is large in employment and financial terms can use the political track to gain protection. Since the concern here is primarily with describing the various means used to convince President Carter that he should help the steel industry, neither the causes of the economic difficulties faced by the industry nor the nature of the trigger price system are analyzed in detail.

As the economy continued its recovery in 1977, the increase in steel output fell short of its predicted level, and employment fell slightly.[14] At the same time the volume of imports rose 35 percent, with the result that the ratio of imports to domestic consumption increased from 14.1 percent to 17.8 percent. Most important was that net income before taxes (and before taking into account the losses of discontinued operations) fell from $2.1 billion in 1976 to $1.1 billion in 1977.[15] The industry viewed the surge in imports as the major cause of its unsatisfactory performance and in turn blamed the rapid rise in imports on the subsidization of steel imports by foreign governments and on unfair pricing practices, specifically dumping, by these producers.[16]

Pressing for countervailing duties to offset the foreign subsidies had the attraction of wide public appeal; however, the practical disadvantage of following this route was that the administration had exercised the option to waive countervailing duties during the period of negotiation on a new international subsidies code, as permitted under the 1974 Trade Act. It was highly unlikely that President Carter would jeopardize the entire negotiation by reversing this policy. At the same time the chances of obtaining import protection by focusing on the charge of foreign dumping— a practice that the American public could also be counted on to condemn—were improved after 1974 because of changes in the antidumping law under the Trade Act of 1974. The basic legal condition for dumping had been the sale of an article for export at less than its market value in the exporter's home market. The 1974 amendment had expanded this definition to include sales of a substantial quantity at less than long-run average costs over an extended period, even if the domestic and export price did not differ.[17] Since pricing at less than average costs is typical during recession periods in industries with large fixed costs, the world steel situation at the time provided an excellent opportunity for U.S. producers to utilize the new dumping law to their protective advantage.

The campaign to convince the public and the administration that some form of restraint on imports was needed involved the use of almost all the techniques of modern lobbying. It began in earnest in late May 1977 with the release of a study conducted for the American Iron and Steel Institute by an economic consulting firm. The report supported the industry's contentions that foreign subsidization and unfair competitive practices did exist and were causing injury to U.S. steel firms. During the Steel Institute's national convention, held at the same time, industry leaders attracted further press coverage by stressing the industry's concern about the domestic impact of rising steel imports. That even these initial efforts were effective is evident from the immediate response of the director of the Office of Management and Budget (OMB), Bert Lance, who said that the administration was interested in the industry's problem, as well as in the reaction shortly after from the chairman of the British steel industry that U.S. countervailing duties on European steel would create utter chaos. Furthermore, by July, Japanese steelmakers had come up with another American-authored study disputing the charges in the institute's study that Japan was selling steel below its production costs.

The most effective means by which public attention was directed to the industry's problems was the well-publicized series of layoffs that began in July and culminated in September with the permanent closing of an old but important steel works in Youngstown, Ohio. In mid-August, Bethlehem Steel announced plans to lay off 7,300 workers in New York and Pennsylvania, including 3,500 in Lackawanna, New York. This was quickly followed by statements from U.S. Steel, Armco Steel, and Lukens Steel stressing the need to release workers in Illinois, Indiana, and Ohio because of competition from foreign steel producers. In September, Youngstown Sheet and Tube Company announced the permanent closing of the Campbell Works plant in Youngstown and the displacement of 5,000 workers. During this two-month period, not a week went by without a series of articles in all the major newspapers and weekly news magazines on the layoff problems. They not only emphasized the plight of the displaced workers but, in areas such as Lackawanna and Youngstown, presented interviews with community leaders who stressed the economic damage to the entire community. The president of the United Steelworkers Union also cooperated in the public relations effort by charging that 60,000 U.S. steelworkers had lost their jobs during the year as a result of increased imports.[18]

The Youngstown closing was further exploited when 250 workers from the area protested at the White House and claimed they had a petition with over 100,000 signatures urging curbs on steel imports. Moreover by closing the Youngstown facility and parts of the Lackawanna plant permanently, company officials not only were able to eliminate these high-cost facilities in a manner that turned the bitterness of workers toward foreign producers rather than toward management, they also dramatized the problems even more by recording significant once-and-for-all losses on their financial statements.

Even the administration of the worker adjustment assistance program tended to validate the claims of the steel industry. The 1974 Trade Act transferred the determination of eligibility to the Labor Department, a government agency whose function is to promote labor's interests, and greatly eased the criteria for assistance. Thus most of the workers displaced at Youngstown and elsewhere were declared eligible for special benefits on the grounds that they were threatened by increased steel imports.

Another important element in any effort to pressure the president into taking trade-restrictive actions is a demand for protection from Congress. The steel industry is one of the industries able to obtain the allegiance of a significant number of congressmen and senators. The steel industry's problems at this time led to a formalization of this commitment by the formation of a Steel Caucus in Congress. This group, initially consisting of 25 senators and 125 congressmen, complained publicly about excessive steel imports and called for import quotas. Their most important accomplishment was securing passage by the Senate of a resolution calling for the vigorous enforcement of the unfair competition laws against foreign steel producers.

Besides using a range of techniques to publicize their problem, the steel companies sought import protection by initiating complaints against foreign producers under various provisions of the law. Earlier efforts to seek assistance in this way had not proved successful. For example, in late 1976, various steel producers had used a shotgun approach in seeking import-restraining actions by the government under both the traditional and new unfair trading practices provisions (section 337 of the 1930 Tariff Act and section 301 of the 1974 Trade Act), under the countervailing duty law, and under the antidumping law. None of the actions resulted in the desired import restraints.[19] However, a dumping complaint against carbon steel plate from Japan filed by a division of Gilmore Steel in March 1977 did result in a decision by Treasury in September that the steel was being sold below Japanese costs. Moreover the ITC subsequently made an affirmative injury finding. Shortly before this decision, U.S. Steel had also filed dumping charges against Japan on a wide variety of products, and the Gilmore decision brought a flood of new dumping complaints. Between that decision and the end of the year, charges of dumping were filed on nearly $1 billion worth of steel imports from Japan, all the major European producers, and India.

By the end of September, the campaign to attract presidential attention to the industry's import problem had succeeded. Senator John Heinz reported on September 22 that President Carter had told Republican senators that he was worried about the shutdowns and layoffs, although he saw no immediate need to grant the industry's demands for import restraints.[20] At a news conference on September 30, the president stated that the layoffs could not be attributed solely to foreign imports, and he described the problems of the industry as "chronic."[21] A news story the next day, however, stated that the administration was considering negotiating temporary steel import quotas.[22] Moreover the article mentioned for the first time the existence of an interagency group headed by the under secretary of the treasury that was considering various import-restraining alternatives. On October 13 Robert Strauss, the U.S. special trade representative, chaired a White House conference of management, labor, and government officials that was also attended by the president. The previous day Strauss had reported that he and the president would seek to ease the steel industry's adjustment to import competition. At the conference itself, the president pledged more vigorous enforcement of fair trade laws to protect U.S. industry from dumping. More specifically he informed the group that within the next month "there will be actions . . . taken to ensure that the present concern about the steel industry is alleviated, not by words or promises but by actions and decisions."[23]

From this and other accounts, it appears that the decision to restrain imports had already been made on the grounds that foreign producers were dumping steel. How to implement such an action raised obvious problems, however, since levying antidumping duties was a second-best outcome for all parties most concerned. The government was fearful that the unilateral imposition of antidumping duties would touch off foreign retaliation and disrupt any ongoing trade negotiations. Domestic firms affected by dumping were not happy with the uncertain impact of antidumping duties, since foreign exporters may still be able to export a substantial volume despite the extra duty. Foreign producers also prefer some other form of import controls. Since they possess monopoly power—or else they would not have been able to engage in price discrimination in the first place—these producers would prefer to charge the higher duty-inclusive domestic price themselves rather than see the government collect the extra duty revenue.

Because of these incentives to seek an alternative solution, many dumping cases are not pursued to the stage of actually imposing antidumping duties. Either the complainant or the alleged dumper works out a mutually agreeable pricing policy whereby the former withdraws the complaint, or some market-sharing arrangement is settled on with the assistance of the government. The antidumping law often serves merely as the vehicle for exerting pressure to bring about one of these outcomes.

In this case, the solution finally agreed on by all parties

was the establishment of minimum prices for steel imports. More specifically, so-called reference prices were established for steel products based on the production costs of the lowest-cost producer (Japan) and including various markups on these costs. Imports entering the country below these prices would trigger an expedited dumping investigation. In other words under the arrangement, there was a presumption that dumping was taking place if imports came into the country at prices below the reference or trigger levels.

For a while the trigger price system worked extremely well for the steel industry. Its formal implementation on February 1, 1978, coincided with a significant increase in economic activity within the country, and by May 1978, the capacity utilization rate in the industry was 94 percent, compared to only 75 percent in December 1977, while the import penetration ratio had fallen from 20 percent to 14 percent between these months. A small number of cases arose in which exporters were accused of shipping at prices below the reference levels, but by and large, foreign producers respected the minimum prices and adjusted their output accordingly. The European Community even introduced a somewhat similar system to deal with its own import problem. In early 1980, however, the periodic increases in the reference prices that were supposedly being made to offset cost increases began to conflict with President Carter's declaration that inflation was now the major economic problem faced by the country. When the administration failed to raise the prices in February 1980, the U.S. Steel Corporation filed broad dumping charges against European producers. The government responded by dismantling the trigger price scheme. A month before the November presidential election, however, President Carter personally announced a new program of governmental assistance to the steel industry that included restoration of the trigger prices at levels 12 percent higher than the ones suspended in March. The new program also included an antisurge provision whereby the government would initiate a dumping investigation if foreign imports exceeded 15.2 percent of domestic consumption and the industry was operating at below 87 percent of capacity.[24] At the same time the steel industry announced that it had withdrawn its dumping complaint against the European producers.

The introduction of the trigger price mechanism for steel imports represented a highly successful lobbying effort by the steel industry. There is no doubt that rapidly rising imports were worsening the industry's economic problems in 1977, and management was concerned about the long-run implications of the import surge. The industry took advantage of these difficulties to announce a series of layoffs that seemed to involve some adjustment to long-run trends as well as to deal with the immediate import problem. It was able to mobilize substantial support in Congress. Thus when President Carter moved to assist the industry, it was in a period when public opinion appeared to demand that he act rather than at a time when he might have appeared to be taking steps to give special treatment to a particular industry.

There does not seem to be anything unique about the steel industry's effort that could not be duplicated by other major U.S. industries under similar circumstances, though perhaps not with such rapid results. However, it also seems evident that the small industries, such as those that produce clothespins, mushrooms, and stainless steel flatware, that typically use a technical track to protection, such as the ITC's import relief mechanism, could not utilize this political approach successfully. The number and geographic dispersion of these firms, as well as the size of their labor force, are not sufficiently large to gain presidential action. Nor does such an industry have the financial or voting power to be able to induce a substantial number of congressmen to pursue its interests in a vigorous manner.

4.5 The Industrial Pattern of U.S. Tariff Reductions in the Tokyo and Kennedy Rounds

In order to allow the United States to enter into new rounds of multilateral trade negotiations, Congress granted the president significant tariff-reducing authority under the Trade Expansion Act of 1962 and the Trade Act of 1974. He was empowered to cut U.S. import duties up to 50 percent under the earlier act and up to 60 percent under the 1974 law. Both laws also gave him the authority to eliminate completely duties of 5 percent or less.

The main purpose of this section is to test the political-economic models of protection set forth in chapter 1 by analyzing the duty cuts across industries that the United States proposed during the Tokyo Round of multilateral trade negotiations (1974–1979). A test of the various models is also undertaken by utilizing information on those tariff items that were completely excluded from duty reductions in the Kennedy Round of trade negotiations (1962–1967). Furthermore both the level of pre-Tokyo Round tariffs across industries and an index of the relative importance of nontariff barriers across industries are analyzed in terms of the various models.

Negotiating Framework

In granting broad duty-reducing authority to the president in 1962 and 1974, Congress specified that he exclude certain products from any duty cuts and, moreover, that he obtain advice from appropriate government agencies and private groups prior to entering into duty-reducing negotiations on the remaining tariff line items. The mandated exceptions were items on which import relief had been given under the ITC route (at the time of the Tokyo Round, these were some ceramic dinnerware, certain ball bearings, stainless and alloy tool steel, nonrubber footwear, color television sets, industrial fasteners, and CB radios) and on which protection had been granted on national security grounds (petroleum). The president was also directed to furnish the ITC with a list of the articles on which duty concessions were being considered and to make offers on these items only after obtaining the advice of the ITC regarding their probable economic effects on domestic industries. Public hearings enabling any interested parties to present their views on the tariff reductions were also necessary prior to making offers to foreign countries. Finally, before entering into any trade agreement, the president was required to seek information and advice from the Departments of Agriculture, Commerce, Defense, Interior, Labor, State, and Treasury, as well as from the Office of the U.S. Special Trade Representative.

The 1974 act mandated substantial input from the private sector. The president was directed to establish an Advisory Committee for Trade Negotiations composed of no more than forty-five representatives of government, labor, industry, agriculture, small business, service industries, retailers, consumer interests, and the general public for the purpose of providing overall policy advice on any trade agreement. In addition he could establish both general advisory committees for industry, labor, and agriculture and sectoral advisory committees designed to give technical advice on various aspects of the trade negotiations. (Presidents Nixon and Carter took advantage of this authority and created an elaborate set of private sector advisory committees.)

As this formal advisory framework makes evident, tariff-reducing decisions at the presidential level were subject to a wide variety of domestic economic and political pressures. Moreover, besides these established mechanisms for bringing to bear the viewpoints of various groups, there were a host of informal means of trying to influence the outcome. For example, various individuals and groups representing particular economic interests often met with officials in different agencies to explain their concerns. They also pressed their views on members of Congress who, in turn, could urge these on the president and key members of his administration. Consequently the actual duty reductions offered by the United States in the Tokyo and Kennedy rounds were the outcome of a complex interactive political process among the White House, different departments in the executive branch, the Congress, and various industries and public interest groups.

The objectives of the other negotiating partners (foreign countries) also played an important part in shaping the nature of the duty reductions, especially in the process of deciding on the average depth of the duty cut. As in the Kennedy Round of negotiations, negotiators in the Tokyo Round agreed on a duty-cutting formula to be followed by all the major participants but from which specific exceptions were permitted. In the Kennedy Round, the rule was simply a 50 percent across-the-board duty reduction. In the Tokyo Round negotiations, however, the European Community successfully pressed for a formula that resulted in larger percentage cuts for high duties than for low duties. Although the average tariff levels on dutiable manufactures were approximately the same in the European Community and the United States, there were more high duties in the latter country, and community officials wanted a duty-cutting formula that would harmonize the distribution of rates in the two trading blocs.

The compromise formula finally settled on was proposed by the Swiss. Letting t be the duty rate on a tariff line item and Δt the change in this duty, the formula was $\Delta t/t = t/(t + 0.14)$. Thus a 14 percent duty was to be cut 50 percent under the formula, whereas a duty of 20 percent was to be reduced 59 percent.[25]

Besides helping to determine the general tariff-cutting rule to be followed in the trade negotiations, other countries influence the pattern of exceptions to the rule. For example, if an important foreign participant presses vigorously for a concession on a particular item, a country might grant a reduction greater than the formula on this item if there is no significant domestic opposition to such an action, or the country might resist domestic pressures not to cut the item at all. The extent to which other countries are willing to provide reciprocity in their tariff-cutting offers also affects the nature of a country's offers. Sometimes a particular participant is unable for domestic political reasons to match the extent of the duty cuts that other countries offer on the country's exports. In that case these other countries generally pull back on their duty-cutting offers on items of particular export interest to that country in order to achieve a rough balance of concessions. Often the withdrawals are on products where domestic pressures against cutting are considerable, but sometimes it is necessary to achieve reciprocity by not cutting on items where there are no special economic or political problems domestically.

Expected Relationships between Industry Characteristics and Duty Reductions

The models set forth in chapter 1 to explain import protection were divided into two general categories. Those in the first group, the common interest or pressure group model and the adding machine model, are based on a view of the political decision-making process that considers the state largely as an intermediary responding to the short-run economic interests of various political groups.

The key point in the common interest group model is that an industry's success in achieving protection by exerting political pressure on elected officials depends on its ability to organize into an effective political pressure group. The ability to overcome the free-rider problem and organize effectively depends in turn on the relative size of firms within the industry and their degree of concentration in output and geographic terms. Low or negative growth rates of employment and output, as well as low or declining profit rates and rising import penetration ratios, also serve to stimulate firms in an industry into organizing for protectionist purposes. The willingness of capitalists and workers to contribute to lobbying organizations is also likely to be negatively related to an industry's value-added share of output. The smaller is the industry's value-added share, the larger will be the percentage change in factor rewards from a given relative change in the price of an industry's output.[26] Consequently industries with low value-added shares are more likely to organize and resist tariff reductions.

The adding machine model also stresses short-run self-interest as the main motivation for protection. Rather than concentrating on the ability of an industry to organize into an effective pressure group, this model assumes that the workers and management in an industry vote as a bloc to promote their short-run economic interests and instead focuses on the relative size of an import-competing industry in employment terms as the key factor influencing the protection decisions of public officials. The model also postulates that the degree of protection is positively related to an import-competing industry's labor-output ratio. Furthermore in contrast to the common interest group model, proponents of the adding machine model believe that industries composed of many small, unconcentrated firms are better able to convince elected officials to promote protection than concentrated sectors composed of a small number of large firms.

The second group of models attempting to explain import protection reject the view that government officials are simply intermediaries who implement the short-run, self-interest aims of various pressure groups. Instead these models can be interpreted as postulating either that private citizens and government officials adopt a long-run view of their self-interest or take into account interpersonal effects and social concerns in reaching decisions about import protection. Three models in this category were distinguished in chapter 1: the status quo model, the social change model, and the foreign policy model.

The status quo model postulates that voters and government officials have a conservative respect for the status quo and accept the income distribution target that any significant absolute reductions in real incomes of any significant groups should be avoided. Government officials implement this social welfare concept during a general trade-liberalizing negotiation by cutting industry duty levels in a manner that minimizes the short-run adjustment costs of workers. Since unskilled, older workers employed in communities where alternative job opportunities are scarce tend to have more difficulty in finding jobs than other workers, one would expect that in a multilateral trade negotiation, tariffs would be cut the least in industries with high proportions of workers who are unskilled, over forty-five years of age, and employed in rural areas. High tariffs should also be cut less than low rates because of officials' conservative respect for the status quo and because a given percentage cut in a high tariff rate generally results in greater competitive pressure than the same reduction in a low tariff rate. In a model that emphasizes the objective of minimizing short-run adjustment costs, one also expects the extent of duty changes across industries to be negatively related to industry growth rates and positively related to changes in import penetration ratios.

The social change model postulates that government officials and many voters seek to promote social goals that go beyond the maintenance of the status quo. They try to bring about changes in the distribution of income and in other socioeconomic relationships. For example, even if there were no differences among workers in their ability to find new jobs, voters and government officials would still want to shield low-income, unskilled workers from the job displacement and wage pressures of increased imports for equity and social justice reasons. Consequently on the basis of this model, one expects duty cuts to be comparatively low in sectors with low average wages, low value added per worker, and a high proportion of unskilled workers. Trade policy actions aimed at fair trade, strengthening the national defense, or promoting a particular life-style also fit into this model.

The last of the three models that emphasize social concerns, the foreign policy model, hypothesizes that government officials and voters view the state as a behavior entity whose economic welfare they wish to promote in its dealings with other states. They adopt a mercantilistic attitude and do not reduce U.S. tariffs on items of special export interest to other countries if these countries do not cut duties on items of special interest to U.S. exporters. A particular application of this theory concerns the developing countries. Since developing countries have been exempted from the requirement that there should be approximate reciprocity among the participants in multilateral trade negotiations, proponents of the international bargaining model expect that the United States (and other developed countries) will not reduce their tariffs very much on items of special interest to the developing countries. It has been suggested that for comparative cost reasons, the developing countries will be particularly interested in reducing duties in the low-wage sectors of U.S. industry. Another implication of the international bargaining model is that U.S. trade officials should be more generous in duty cuts of interest to other countries when U.S. foreign direct investment is relatively high in these countries.

In testing the various hypotheses derived from the different models, it is necessary to include variables that control for the manner in which an industry's comparative cost position influences the perceived need for protection. Specifically industries in which the ratio of exports to production is high and the import penetration ratio is low are not likely to be perceived as needing protection either by government officials or the management and labor force of the industry.

Another problem in trying to determine the relative explanatory power of the various models is that the same variable is sometimes used by the different formulators of the models to serve as a proxy to capture quite different behavioral patterns. For example, the level of wages across industries is utilized as a relevant independent variable in both the social change and foreign policy models. Similarly proponents of both the status quo and social change models claim that the proportion of unskilled workers is a relevant proxy for testing their model.

A number of other factors besides the ones emphasized by the different models affect the extent of duty cuts across industries in a multilateral trade negotiation. Pressures by other countries for tariffs on particular items to be reduced have already been mentioned. Such factors as the relative political strength of the president in areas where an industry is located or the special ties of the industry to key leaders in Congress or the executive branch may also affect the depth of tariff cut offered by U.S. negotiators. Personality differences among presidents, key congressional and executive branch leaders, and industry officials can also play an important role in the outcome of trade policy decisions. Furthermore, dynamic interactions among various unique historical events may influence the ability of an industry to secure protection. The focus here is on testing whether various structural characteristics of U.S. industries affect the depth of tariff reductions. While many other factors may shape the patterns of industry cuts, it will be assumed that these factors do not systematically bias the relationships postulated in the different models.

Table 4.2 summarizes the expected relationships between the extent of tariff cuts across industries in a multilateral tariff-reducing negotiation and various key industry characteristics selected to reflect behavioral motivations in the two models that stress the short-run self-interest of economic agents and the three models that emphasize social concerns. Levels of protection across industries should also be related in the same manner to most of the same industry characteristics. For example, since the cuts in tariff rates are entered in the regressions as negative numbers, one would expect growth rates of employment and output to be negatively related to the tariff changes on the basis of both the pressure group and status quo models. Similarly low tariff levels should be associated with high growth rates.

Empirical Results

The first set of tariff cuts used to test the various models are those that the United States offered in the Tokyo

Table 4.2
Expected relationships between key industry characteristics and tariff changes and levels of protection

Industry characteristic	Various models (expected relationships)					
	Pressure group	Adding machine	Status quo	Social change	Foreign policy	Comparative cost controls
1. Seller and geographic concentration ratios	Positive	Negative				
2. Number of firms	Negative					
3. Growth rate	Negative		Negative			
4. Change in import penetration ratio	Positive		Positive			
5. Extent of foreign investment	Negative				Negative	
6. Value-added share of output	Negative					
7. Number of workers		Positive				
8. Labor-output coefficient		Positive		Positive		
9. Proportion of unskilled workers			Positive	Positive		
10. Average wage				Negative	Negative	
11. Import penetration ratio						Positive
12. Historical level of protection			Positive			

Round. They are not the actual reductions finally agreed on—and thus exclude final pull-backs for reciprocity reasons—but they do take into consideration the initial requests of other countries for specific concessions.

The tariff cuts offered on the approximately 5,000 manufactured tariff line items were classified into 292 four-digit manufacturing industries on the basis of the Standard Industrial Classification (SIC) system of the United States.[27] Two different variations of the tariff cut were employed as dependent variables: the rate of decline in duties collected and the difference in the tariff rate given by the agreed-on Swiss formula and the tariff rate offered by the United States.[28] The various industry characteristics utilized as proxies for the different types of economic-political variables were either taken from the data bank of the ITC and other sources or constructed from data presented in various government documents.[29] It proved possible to obtain information on many but not all of the variables mentioned in the discussion of expected relationships.

The results of regressing different measures of the Tokyo Round cuts on various industry characteristics are reported in tables 4.3 and 4.5. Table 4.4 explains the abbreviations used for the independent variables in the tables and their sources. In some of the regressions, the models are tested using only tariff rates that initially were above 5 percent, and in one case the cuts are regressed against only the characteristics of industries with net import deficits. Rates below 5 percent are excluded to determine if the relationships were biased by the U.S. negotiating tactic of cutting rates below 5 percent more than the formula cut as a means of achieving a reasonably deep average cut.

The regression analysis of duty reductions offered by the United States indicates that the industries receiving relatively low duty cuts are ones in which workers tend to be unskilled and low paid. These industries are also charac-

Table 4.3
Relationship between U.S. Tokyo Round tariff cuts for manufactured goods and various industry characteristics

Independent variables and expected signs[a]	All industries	Industries in which exports < imports	Industries in which $t > .05$
CONR8L70 (+)	−.65(−3) (−.79)		
NOFIRMS (−)			−.14(−4) (−.48)
FDI1 (−)	.99(+1) (2.05)**		
DTEMPL (−)			−.11 (−1.77)*
DP70-76 (−)	−.24(−1) (−.79)	−.55(−1) (−1.05)	
IMPENRAC (+)	.26 (.65)	.15(+1) (2.55)***	.30(−1) (4.40)**
VSH 76 (−)		.11 (.48)	−.14 (−1.34)
TEMPL70 (+)			.51(−3) (2.66)***
TOTCAP70 (+)	.62(−5) (.93)		
PAY 76 (−)			−.13 (−2.87)***
SKUNSK 70 (+)	.97 (3.19)***	.12(+1) 2.30***	
LQ 76 (+)		−.33(+1) (−1.18)	
LNIMPENR (+)	.54(−2) (.44)	.50(−1) (1.87)*	.30(−1) (4.40)***
TLEVEL (?)	−.13 (−.40)	.90(−2) (.03)	
NTBUS (+)	.30(−1) (1.75)*	.29(−1) (2.48)***	
Constant	−.81	−.74	−.11
Adjusted R^2	.10	.17	.18
F ratio	3.42	3.07	6.91

Notes: The dependent variable is the average rate of duty reduction and is entered into the equations as a negative number. The t statistic is in the parentheses below the regression coefficients; the number in the parentheses beside the coefficients indicates the direction and number of digits the decimal point should be moved.

a. See table 4.4 for an explanation and the source of the independent variables.

*Significant at the 10 percent level.   **Significant at the 5 percent level.
***Significant at the 1 percent level.

Table 4.4
Definition and sources of independent variables

Variables from the ITC's "Industrial Characteristics and Trade Performance" Databank (some updated)	
CONR4L70	Concentration ratio, 1970: percentage of shipments accounted for by the four largest firms in the industry
CONR8L70	Concentration ratio, 1970: percentage of shipments accounted for by the eight largest firms in the industry
HCAP67	Human capital measure, 1967: difference, capitalized at 10 percent, between the annual average industry wage per employee and the average wage for persons with less than eight years' education ($2,191)
IMPENR67	Import penetration ratio, 1967: imports divided by shipments plus imports minus exports
IMPENR70	Import penetration ratio, 1970
IMPENRAC	Absolute change in the import penetration ratio, 1965–1970
LABINT67	Labor intensity ratio, 1967: payroll divided by value added
LABINT70	Labor intensity ratio, 1970
NTBUS	Index of incidence of nontariff barriers in the United States, 1970
PRODWK67	Production workers, 1967: thousands of persons
PRODWK70	Production workers, 1970: thousands of persons
PRODWK76	Production workers, 1976: thousands of persons
SKILLD70	Skills measure, 1970: professional and kindred workers, plus managers and administrators (except farm), plus craftsmen and kindred workers, as percentage of total employment. Based on three-digit SIC data, with values repeated at four-digit levels
SKLPC	Skill-research measure, 1970: percentage of scientists and engineers engaged in R&D times the total employment of scientists and engineers, divided by total employment
SKUNSK70	Basic labor ratio, 1970: ratio of ($2,669 times total employment) to total payroll, where $2,669 is the average wage of persons with less than eight years' education

Table 4.4 (Continued)

TEMPL70	Total employment, 1970: thousands of persons
TOTCAP70	Total capital stock, 1970: millions of dollars
YSALRA68	Ratio of gross profits to sales for firms with annual sales over $1 million, 1968
XDV70	Ratio of U.S. exports to the value of shipments, 1970

Variables constructed from the ITC Databank (some updated)

LQ 76	=	PRODWK76/VALADD76, where VALADD76 is value added, 1976: millions of dollars
DP70-76	=	(VALADD76 − PRODWG76) − (VALADD70 − PRODWG70) / TOTCAP70, where PRODWG76 and PRODWG70 are production worker wage bills, 1976 and 1970, respectively
DTEMPL	=	(TEMPL70 − TEMPL65) / TEMPL65, where TEMPL70 and TEMPL65 are total employment, 1970 and 1965: thousands of persons
LNIMPENR	=	ln (IMPENR70)
VSH 76	=	VALADD76/TSHIP76, where TSHIP76 is the value of shipments, 1976: millions of dollars
PAY 76	=	TPAYRL76/TEMPL76

Other variables

FTAX 74	Foreign tax credits in 1974, thousands of dollars. (Source: Department of the Treasury, *Statistics of Income 1974*)
FDI1	FTAX74 divided by total assets, 1974. (Source: Department of the Treasury, *Statistics of Income 1974*)
FDI2	FTAX74 divided by depreciable assets, 1974. (Source: Department of the Treasury, *Statistics of Income 1974*)
NOFIRMS	Number of firms in the industry, 1977. (Source: U.S. Department of Commerce, Bureau of the Census, *1977 Census of Manufactures*)
TLEVEL	Average tariffs, 1976
NTBUS	Index of incidence of nontariff barriers in the United States, 1970.

Table 4.5
Relationship between U.S. Tokyo Round tariff cuts for manufactured goods and various industry characteristics

Independent variables and expected signs[a]	All industries	All industries	Industries in which $t > .05$	All industries
CONR4L70 (−)				−.37(−4) (−.50)
FDI2 (+)		−.17(−5) (−.98)	−.94(−1) (−.34)	
DP70-76 (+)				.39(−4) (0)
PRODWK70 (−)	−.39(−4) (−1.74)*			
PRODWK76 (−)				−.39(−4) (−1.61)
SKUNSK70 (−)				−.73(−1) (−3.46)***
SKILLD70 (+)	.51(−1) (3.11)***	.60(−1) (2.92)***	.46(−1) (1.48)	

	(1)	(2)	(3)	(4)
LNIMPENR70 (−)		−.23(−2)		−.14(−2)
		(−2.94)***		(−1.58)
IMPENR70 (−)	−.26(−1)		−.26(−2)	
	(−2.23)**		(−1.93)**	
TLEVEL (−)	−.30	−.32	−.41	−.28
	(−13.45)***	(−12.44)***	(−10.41)***	(−10.67)***
NTBUS (−)	−.15(−2)	−.46(−2)	.32(−2)	−.24(−2)
	(−2.26)**	(−3.58)***	(1.49)	(−3.12)***
Constant	.93(−2)	.19(−2)	−.13(−1)	.47(−1)
Adjusted R^2	.54	.61	.65	.56
F ratio	25.48	74.97	58.08	44.01

Notes: The dependent variable is the difference between the rate given by the Swiss formula and the offered rate. The t statistic is in the parentheses below the coefficient; the number in the parentheses beside the coefficient indicates the direction and number of digits the decimal point should be moved.

a. See table 4.4 for an explanation and the sources of the independent variables.

*Significant at the 10 percent level.

**Significant at the 5 percent level.

***Significant at the 1 percent level.

terized by a large number of workers, slow employment growth, high and rising import penetration ratios, and high levels of protection.

Proponents of each of the different models can claim some support from these results; however, some models fare better than others. For example, variables such as the degree of firm concentration and the number of firms in an industry, that proponents of the pressure group model suggest for capturing the ability of an industry to overcome the free rider problem and organize effectively—the key point in this model—are not significant. In contrast, performance variables such as employment growth and changes in an industry's import penetration ratio that indicate the incentive to organize are significant in the expected direction; however, these latter variables are also used in the status quo model to reflect the ability of workers in an industry to adjust to an increase in imports.

The adding machine model scores somewhat better in that its key variable, number of workers in an industry, is sometimes statistically significant with the expected sign; however, neither the coefficient on the labor-intensity variable nor that on the firm concentration variable is significant.[30]

The status quo model performs well. Various measures of the relative importance of unskilled workers in an industry invariably turn out to be significantly related to the depth of the tariff. Furthermore the model receives additional support due to the significance of the growth rate of employment and the change in a sector's import penetration ratio.

The effects of including the level of industry tariffs and the incidence of nontariff barriers, other key variables of the status quo model, are interesting. In table 4.3 where the dependent variable is the average tariff reduction in each industry, the sign on the tariff variable is negative in the all-industry case but positive for only net importing industries as well as for industries with tariffs above 5 percent (not shown in the table).[31] None of the tariff coefficients is statistically significant, however, even though the formula agreed on reduces high duties relatively more than low duties. The reluctance on the part of government officials to reduce high duties significantly, as hypothesized in the status quo model, largely offsets this harmonization objective. The tendency to maintain the status quo is seen clearly in table 4.5, where the dependent variable is the difference between the tariff rate given by applying the formula and by the rate actually offered. The coefficient on the tariff level variable is highly significant in the negative direction, indicating that the extent to which the tariff rate given by the formula was lower than the actual new rate offered increased at higher and higher tariff levels. The tariff variable is also significantly negative when the dependent variable is the proportion of the formula cut actually offered (not included in the tables).

The tariff level and the incidence of nontariff barriers provide by far the greatest explanation of the duty cuts across industries when, as in table 4.5, the duty-cut variable is the difference between the tariff rate given by the agreed-upon cutting formula and the actual tariff rate offered. The R^2 for equations that exclude the tariff-level variable but include various combinations of the other independent variables invariably falls below .1 (not shown in table 4.5). Although the tariff level variable is not significant in table 4.3 where the average duty cut is the dependent variable, the fact that high duties were not cut more in percentage terms, as would have been the case if the duty-cutting rule had been followed, indicates the pressures against significantly cutting high duty items.

This pressure against cutting high duty items significantly also extended to those sectors where the incidence of non-tariff barriers was high.

The average wage level by industry and the relative importance of unskilled workers—two variables used in testing the social change model—are invariably significant in the expected direction. Since the skill variable is also used in testing the status quo model and is highly correlated with the wage variable, it is difficult to determine whether the correlations reflect a desire by government officials to minimize adjustment costs or to raise the living standards of low-income workers relative to others. It may be that in trade negotiations, government officials try to maintain the status quo position for most workers but go beyond this for low-income workers to try to improve their short-run relative position. The use of the wage variable in the foreign policy model as a proxy for products of export interest to the developing countries causes similar problems of interpretation; however, the foreign investment variable, also used in testing this model, is either not significant or significant with the wrong sign.

The variables included in the regression to control for comparative cost conditions give mixed results. The import penetration ratio is almost always significant in the expected manner—high import ratios are associated with low duty cuts—but the export-shipments ratio is not significant, although it has the predicted sign. Perhaps this is another indication of the comparative ineffectiveness of export interests for lobbying purposes. Excluding industries with an export surplus from the regressions also does not have much effect on the R^2 or the significance of the coefficients.

The results from examining data on tariff reductions in the Kennedy Round of multilateral negotiations, as well as data on the pattern of pre-Tokyo Round tariff levels and

Table 4.6
Relationship between exceptions from Kennedy Round tariff cuts and various industry characteristics

Independent variables and expected signs[a]	Dependent variable: (1) no cut; (0) cut	
LABINT67 (+)	1.68	
	(2.20)***	
IMPENR67 (+)	4.18	7.80
	(2.61)**	(3.33)***
HCAP67 (−)	−.27(−4)	−.31(−4)
	(−2.97)***	(−4.21)***
SKLPC (−)	−.22	
	(−1.91)*	
YSALRA68 (−)		9.54
		(1.81)*
PRODWK67 (+)	.54(−2)	.63(−2)
	(2.11)**	(2.58)**
Likelihood ratio statistic	41.34	36.71

Notes: The t statistic is in the parentheses below the coefficient; the number in the parentheses beside the coefficient indicates the direction and number of digits the decimal point should be moved.
a. Explanations and sources of the independent variables are given in table 4.4.
*Significant at the 10 percent level.
**Significant at the 5 percent level.
***Significant at the 1 percent level.

the incidence of nontariff barriers, are presented in tables 4.6 and 4.7. In table 4.6 the political-economic features of four-digit SIC industries in which at least 5 percent of the duty line items were not reduced at all are compared with the characteristics of those industries in which less than 5 percent of the tariff line items were excluded from cuts. The results of this probit analysis are generally similar to those for the Tokyo Round cuts.[32] The exclusions tended to be concentrated in sectors where skill levels were low, em-

Table 4.7
Relationship between U.S. tariff level and nontariff trade barriers and various industry characteristics

Independent variables and expected signs[a]	Dependent variable: U.S. tariff levels in manufacturing		Dependent variable: Index of NTBs in manufacturing	
CONR8L70 (+)	.15(−3) (.74)			.18(−3) (.05)
CORN4L70 (+)		.26(−3) (1.39)		−.47(−2) (−.81)
NOFIRMS (−)	−.46(−5) (−2.13)**		−.32(−5) (−1.97)*	
FDI1 (−)			.11(+1) (1.04)	.32(+2) (1.51)
DTEMPL (−)	.84(−2) (.5)	.71(−2) (.43)		
DP70-76 (−)			−.52(−1) (−.38)	−.48 (−.90)
VSH76 (−)		−.42(−2) (−1.89)*	.51(−1) (1.60)	.35 (5.39)***
TEMPL70 (+)	.94(−4) (1.73)*	.28(−4) (.62)		.20(−2) (1.37)
TOTCAP70 (+)				.82(−4) (2.88)***
LABINT70 (+)	.19(−1) (.57)	.22(−1) (.66)		−.35(+1) (−3.41)***

PAY76 (−)	−.16(−1) (−10.95)***				
SKUNSK70 (+)		−.15(−1) (−10.71)***	.14 (1.68)*	.59(+1) (4.72)***	
LQ 76 (+)			.33(−1) (10.88)***		
LNIMPENR70 (+)		.35(−2) (1.75)*		−.66(−1) (−1.23)	.50(−1) (.66)
IMPENR70 (+)			−.20(−1) (−.60)		
IMPENRAC (+)				−.36(+1)* (−2.06)	
XDV70 (−)	.34(−1) (.52)	.33(−1) (.82)			−.27(+1) (−2.22)**
TLEVEL (+)				.24(+1) (1.63)	.55(+1)*** (3.33)
NTBUS (+)	.46(−2) (2.24)**	.48(−2) (2.32)**	.61(−2) (2.04)*		
Constant	.26	.24	.15(−1)	.23(+1)	.22(+1)
Adjusted R^2	.39	.38	.51	.23	.18
F ratio	16.29	17.34	27.32	7.92	7.57

Notes: The t statistic is in the parentheses below the coefficient; the number in the parentheses beside the coefficient indicates the direction and number of digits the decimal point should be moved.

a. Explanations and sources of the independent variables are given in table 4.4.

*Significant at the 10 percent level.   **Significant at the 5 percent level.   ***Significant at the 1 percent level.

ployment was high, labor's share of value added was high, and the import penetration ratio was high.

The average ratio of duties collected to the value of the dutiable imports has declined more than 80 percent (from a level of nearly 60 percent) in the United States over the last fifty years, and consequently existing interindustry differences in tariff rates have been closely related to the differential ability of industries to resist this general downward pressure on tariffs. Since comparative conditions of profitability have changed considerably among industries over this period, however, it would not be expected that recent changes in such variables as employment or the import penetration level would necessarily be correlated with duty levels. The existence of two-way relationships between an industry's ability to obtain protection and the magnitude of the various independent variables is also a serious problem in dealing with tariff levels. For example, a low import penetration ratio may be associated with a high tariff level precisely because the industry has been successful in obtaining protection.

Table 4.7 yields relationships on protection levels generally similar to those found in analyzing duty cuts. Industries with low wages, a high proportion of unskilled workers, and a high labor/output ratio tend to be highly protected—relationships that support the social change model and to some extent the status quo model. The regressions also give support to the adding machine model, since the employment and labor/output ratio variables are significant in some runs. Furthermore while the degree of firm concentration is still not significant, one of the key variables of the pressure group model, number of firms in an industry, is significantly related to tariff levels in a negative manner. Both of the comparative cost variables, the degree of import penetration and extent of export orientation across industries, are also significantly associated with the level of tariffs in some regressions. Industries that are highly protected by tariffs are also highly protected by nontariff barriers. Compared with tariff protection, however, industries with significant nontariff protection tend to be larger in capital-stock terms, less labor intensive, less using of intermediate inputs, and less export oriented.

As the preceding analysis of Tokyo Round and Kennedy Round duty cuts and pre–Tokyo Round levels of tariffs and the incidence of nontariff barriers across industries indicates, the problem is not one of finding statistically significant relationships but in distinguishing among the different models in terms of their explanatory power. The fact that the same variables are suggested as proxies by the formulators of the different models makes it very difficult to delineate the different behavior patterns.

One conclusion that does seem warranted, however, is that the short-run self-interest framework is insufficient to account for the variations in tariff cuts and tariff levels across industries. Since unskilled, low-income workers are poor pressure group organizers and advocates, the significant negative relationship between these variables and the magnitude of duty cuts and duty levels strongly suggests that demands from pressure groups based on short-run self-interest are insufficient to explain protection reductions and protection levels. Formulations such as the status quo and social change models, which stress that voters and government officials are motivated in their trade policy decisions by long-run self-interest or interpersonal effects and broad social concerns, are also needed to explain trade policies.

The two-stage least-squares regressions reported in table 4.8 attempt to compare the relative importance of demands by pressure groups for protection and the willingness of government officials to supply protection. First

Table 4.8
Two-stage least-squares analysis of U.S. duty reduction in the Tokyo Round

Independent variables and expected signs in columns 2–5[a] (1)	Demand equation (2)	Reduced form demand and supply equations			
		All industries[b,d] (3)	Industries where t>.05[b,d] (4)	All industries[b,e] (5)	All industries[c,e] (6)
DEMAND (+)		.14(+1) (.64)	.36(−1) (1.86)*	.37(−1) (1.05)	−.56 (−1.90)*
IMPENRAC (+)	.14(+1) (.45)	.11 (.30)	.16 (.47)	.88(−1) (.24)	−.92(−1) (−.03)
DTEMPL (−)	.14 (.24)				
DP70-76 (−)		.57(−2) (.08)	.60 (.94)	−.15(−1) (−.21)	−.16 (−.27)
IMPEN70 (+)	.29(+1) (2.11)**	.27 (1.50)	.19 (1.02)	.31 (1.73)*	−.26(+1) (−1.73)*
NOFIRMS (−)	−.10(−3) (−.85)				
CONR4L70 (+)	.75(−2) (1.03)				
VSH76 (−)	−.30(+1) (−2.262)***				
LABINT70 (+)	.41 (2.78)***				

	(1)	(2)	(3)	(4)	(5)
FDI1 (−)	.67(+1) (.17)				
XDV70 (−)	−.62 (−2.69)***				
TEMPL76 (+)		.37(−3) (1.86)*	.24(−3) (1.46)	.35(−3) (1.76)*	−.47(−3) (−.29)
SKUNSK (+)		.93 (3.42)***	.44 (1.96)*	1.00 (3.73)***	−.38 (−.17)
TLEVEL (+ or ?)	.12(+2) (5.18)***	−.32 (−.74)	−.25 (−.67)	−.14 (−.42)	−.86(+1) (−3.18)***
Constant	−.23(+1) (−2.40)**	−.81 (−7.61)***	−.59 (−6.55)***	−.87 (−9.72)***	−.29(+1) (4.01)***
Maximum log likelihood ratio	92.26				
Adjusted R^2		.12	.15	.12	.11
F ratio		3.78	3.49	3.89	3.38

Notes: The number in the parentheses beside the coefficients indicates the direction and number of digits the decimal point should be moved, while the number in the parentheses below the coefficients is the ratio of the maximum likelihood estimate to the standard error in the demand equation and the t statistic in the other equations.

a. See table 4.4 for an explanation and the sources of the independent variables.

b. The dependent variable is the rate of duty reduction.

c. The dependent variable is the proportion of the formula cut offered.

d. The demand variable is the values predicted from the maximum likelihood coefficients of the demand equation. Using the predicted values of testifying instead yields generally similar results.

e. The demand variable is a dummy indicating whether the industry actually did (1) or did not (0) testify against the trade bill.

*Significant at the 10 percent level.   **Significant at the 5 percent level.   ***Significant at the 1 percent level.

it was postulated that the intensity of an industry's demand for protection could be measured by a binary variable indicating whether the industry did or did not testify against the Trade Act of 1974 during the House and Senate committee hearings on the bill. Specifically it was assumed that there was some threshold level of demand for protection above which an industry would have come forward to oppose the bill and below which it either would not testify at all or would testify in favor of the proposed duty cuts. Thus, in the probit model utilized, if an industry testified against the bill, it was assigned a 1; if it did not, it was assigned a 0.[33] The independent variables used to estimate whether the threshold demand level was or was not reached are indicated in column 2 of table 4.8.

As column 2 in the table shows, all but two of the ten variables have the expected signs, and five of the ten are significant in the expected direction. The industries asking for protection were ones for which the tariff level was already high, exports were only a small fraction of shipments, the import penetration was high, the ratio of the value added to total shipments was low, and labor's share of value added was high.

The second-stage regressions results are presented in columns 3 and 4. The variable to be explained is the rate of tariff reductions offered across industries in the Tokyo Round. One of the independent variables used in explaining these duty reductions is the numerical value predicted for each industry from the maximum likelihood coefficients listed in column 2 for the demand equation. The predicted values are interpreted as indicating the intensity of the demand for protection by each industry. The other independent variables listed in columns 3 and 4 are then interpreted as reflecting the willingness of government officials to supply protection for an industry in the form of relatively low duty cuts (or no cuts at all).

In columns 5 and 6 the industry value entered for the demand variable is not based on a prior regression equation but is simply the dummy value indicating whether the industry did (1) or did not (0) testify against the 1974 Trade Act. Furthermore the dependent variable in the equation reported in the last column is the proportion of the formula cut that was offered by the United States, whereas the dependent variable in columns 3, 4, and 5 is the rate by which tariffs were reduced. The expected sign on the tariff level coefficient is negative when the proportion of formula cut is the dependent variable whereas the expected sign on the tariff level variable is ambiguous when the rate of duty reduction is the dependent variable. Furthermore for the first measure of the duty reductions, the expected signs on the rest of the variables are the opposite to what is expected for the second measure of the reductions.

As the coefficients on the demand variable indicate, the intensity of the demand for protection does play a significant role in influencing duty reductions across industries when only industries with tariff levels above 5 percent are included as well as when the measure of the cut is the proportion of the formula cut offered. However, considerations such as the relative importance of unskilled labor, the existing levels of tariffs, and the size of the labor force in each industry—all factors that reflect the willingness of government officials to provide protection for status quo, social change, and voting pressure reasons—are also important.[34]

It seems impossible at this stage of empirical testing to determine more precisely the explanatory power of the different models. To do so, it is necessary to find economic variables that delineate the models more sharply and thereby reduce the overlaps that now exist.

Consider, for example, the common interest or pressure group hypothesis. This model assumes that if an industry organizes into a pressure group, it will secure higher levels of protection. The ability of an industry to organize depends, in turn, on the degree of concentration and the number of firms in the industry. In the empirical tests undertaken, however, the degree of concentration was not found to be significantly related to protection, and the number of firms was significant only in the case of tariff levels (in contrast to tariff cuts). It may be that overcoming the free rider problem is not as difficult as the pressure group model postulates, especially when the behavior framework is widened to include both the type of altruism noted by Arrow (1975), in which individuals in an industry recognize an implicit social contract to behavior toward others in the industry in a manner calculated to help all members, and the participation effect stressed by Kau and Rubin (1982). When a rising import penetration ratio coupled with slow growth threatens to cause substantial losses and reductions in employment in an industry, the typical member of the industry is likely to recognize the importance of this type of altruistic behavior from a long-run self-interest viewpoint and to become willing to participate in the collective action of lobbying. Furthermore, if the owner of a small firm in the industry perceives the injury-causing import increase to be due to some unfair trade practice on the part of foreign countries, he may contribute to the lobbying effort because of the satisfaction he gains from participating in a collective effort to promote a desirable social goal, that is, taking offsetting action against unfair trade practices.

Of particular interest about organized pressure groups is whether they do in fact succeed in obtaining protection and how the forms of lobbying vary depending on the structure of an industry. Consequently we need to relate direct measures of political pressures across industries to the extent to which protectionist outcomes are achieved in these sectors. Although there is no single ideal index of political pressure and difficult data collection problems exist in the field, regressing tariff levels or duty cuts on such indicators of active political pressure as the size of lobbying expenditures and political contributions by an industry, the extent to which members of an industry make their views known to government officials through letters or personal visits, the volume of testimony and public statements in favor of the industry's position, and so forth would seem to be a better way of testing the model than relating tariff levels to such variables as concentration ratios and the number of firms.

There are also more direct measures available for testing most of the other models. As Bale (1977) has shown, the actual magnitude of adjustment costs (in terms of forgone income) associated with a given reduction in protection can be estimated for each industry. Similarly instead of using partial and imperfect indicators of comparative costs such as average wages (as in the foreign policy model), it is possible to utilize estimates of revealed comparative costs based either directly on a country's trade performance or on differences in factor prices inferred from this performance.[35] Furthermore the willingness of other nations to offer trading concessions in return for concessions granted by others could be measured directly on a sector-by-sector basis by examining the offers of various participants in a trade negotiation.

While collection of the data needed to come up with these kinds of direct measures of the behavior characterizing the various models is a formidable task, such an effort seems to be required if we are to make significant further progress in understanding the political-economic determinants of the structure of protection. Currently we are able to predict this structure reasonably well from various industry characteristics, but we do not fully understand what type of political and economic behavior these variables reflect.

4.6 Summary

This chapter has traced changes in the president's trade policy powers, examined likely behavior of the president on trade issues in more detail than was done in chapter 1, and tested various hypotheses concerning this behavior. The hypothesis testing was conducted by considering presidential actions in affirmative ITC import injury cases, by examining the interactions among the president, Congress, and private industry in the implementation of the trigger price mechanism for the steel industry, and by analyzing the duty reductions across industries in two multilateral trade negotiations as well as the tariff levels in these sectors.

The major theme in the discussion of the president's powers to control imports is that while Congress has periodically granted the president's requests for additional tariff-cutting authority, it has also endeavored over the years to modify the trade policy powers of the chief executive in such a way as to make U.S. international commercial policy more responsive to its wishes.

The analysis of presidential actions in affirmative ITC import injury decisions is consistent with a number of the hypotheses suggested about presidential behavior. For example, the president's greater willingness to accept affirmative ITC findings when his decisions are due near the time of a congressional or presidential election or when Congress is about to take legislative action on another trade policy issue that is important to the president supports the pressure group model of political action. However, the absence of a statistically significant relationship between his decisions and whether Congress requests the investigation, as well as whether labor initiates the petition, does not support this model. Nor does the lack of a strong relationship between the size of an industry in employment terms and the president's decisions support the adding machine model. The tendency for the president to reject ITC affirmative findings in periods when the inflation rate is rising suggests that more than pressure group or industry voting strength politics are involved in the president's import relief decisions. Another interesting finding is that the proportion of commissioners who favor import relief in a particular case is not significantly correlated with whether the president also favors import relief.

The discussion of the interactions among the president, representatives of the steel industry, and members of Congress at the time the steel industry was granted protection through the trigger price mechanism is included in the chapter to show how a political track to protection is sometimes followed. To be able to apply political pressure directly as well as indirectly on the president, an industry must possess significant resources in financial terms or in terms of voting strength. These must be used to convince the president not only of the merits of the case but that voters in general will support his protective action and that he will lose needed political support from many members of Congress on other issues if he does not grant protection. The implementation of the trigger price mechanism for the steel industry illustrates these points very well and lends support to the pressure group and adding machine models.

Data on the industry pattern of tariff cuts in the Tokyo and Kennedy rounds, as well as on the level of tariffs across industries, provide the opportunity to use regression analysis to test the various political-economic models of trade policy behavior. The results of this analysis support each of the models to some extent, with the status quo model performing especially well. But the overlap in the various proxies suggested by the formulators of the models to measure different behavior patterns makes it very difficult to assess the relative explanatory powers of the various models. It is necessary to find variables that distinguish the models more sharply before progress toward this goal can be made.

Nevertheless, one broad conclusion that does seem warranted on the basis of the analyses undertaken is that the models focusing exclusively on short-run, direct self-interest are insufficient for explaining the wide range of behavior patterns observable in the trade policy area. Models that include behavior based either on long-run self-interest or concern for the welfare of other groups and the state are also necessary to account for the actions of voters and public officials. While not focused on in this study, differences among public officials in personality, background, and experience also play an important role in determining the nature of public policy decisions.

5

Conclusions and Policy Recommendations

5.1 Trade Policy Behavior

The purpose of this study has been to contribute to a better understanding of the manner in which U.S. import policies are formed and implemented. Traditionally most economists have taken such policies as exogenously determined, even though they have long recognized that there is a two-way relationship between changes in economic variables and changes in economic policies. In recent years, however, a growing number of economists have concluded that economic tools and an economic way of thinking are useful for analyzing the operation of political markets as well as economic markets. This has led to the development of the theory of public choice.

In utilizing the public choice framework to analyze U.S. import policies, hypotheses based on a number of different political economy models of behavior were set forth and tested statistically and by examining their consistency with particular trade policy events. Trade policy decisions in three government units were analyzed: the Congress, the ITC, and the executive branch. A description of existing trade policy powers within these government units and how they have changed over the last fifty years or so was also given.

Two main groups of political economy models deal with import policy. One set regards the government simply as an intermediary responding to political pressures from various groups whose members are attempting to maximize their short-run gains from trade by influencing public policy. The pressures on elected officials take such forms as withdrawing funds and manpower assistance in election campaigns and failing to support officials at the polls.

The second set of models is consistent with the view that voters and government officials are motivated either by long-run economic self-interest that is consistent with some short-run concern for others or by a general concern for others based on interpersonal utility relationships or certain ethical standards. Government officials are also regarded as having some scope to follow their own public policy preferences.

The main conclusion of the study is that both sets of models are needed to explain trade policy behavior by government officials. For example, although the market structure variables stressed in the pressure group model do not seem to be significant in determining which industries are most successful in securing protection, there is little doubt that political pressures exerted on government officials by common-interest groups affect political behavior on trade policy issues. Regression analysis of the voting record of members of Congress on the 1974 Trade Act is consistent with this view. The larger was the proportion of the industrial labor force in each congressional district or state employed in import-sensitive industries, the greater was the likelihood that the member of Congress representing the district or state voted against this legislation. Not unexpectedly, however, export-oriented sectors were not equally successful in securing votes in favor of the 1974 Trade Act.

The fact that tariff rates were cut less in the Tokyo Round

on the products of industries testifying against congressional approval of the Trade Act of 1974 than on the products of industries not doing so is also supportive of the pressure group framework. Still another piece of evidence supporting the view that the voting power of a pressure group influences trade policy decisions is the correlation (though not always significant) in the expected direction between the size of an industry in employment terms and the depth of industry duty cuts in the Tokyo Round.

The episode involving the extension of the period during the Tokyo Round negotiation when the president could waive the imposition of countervailing duties further illustrates how politically powerful, import-sensitive industries are able to obtain promises of protection from the president. The manner in which the steel industry gained import protection in 1978 in the form of the trigger price mechanism is another example of the effectiveness of political pressures by a major industry. The president also seems more receptive to approving affirmative ITC escape clause cases just before an election.

Yet if present trade policy behavior by public officials is entirely explainable by the political pressure models, one would expect much more protection than actually now exists. Analysis of the behavior of groups favoring liberal trade policies indicates they are generally less effective politically than protectionist groups, especially in opposing protection for specific industries rather than general protection. Therefore a problem for advocates of the pressure group framework is to explain why we do not now have very high levels of protection across industries, such as those that were imposed under the Smoot-Hawley Tariff Act of 1930.

The answer seems to be that certain institutional changes were made after 1930 in the protection-setting process that significantly reduced the ability of pressure

groups to influence protection levels in particular industries. These changes involved, first, giving the president
the authority to modify tariff levels on particular items
within a certain range and, second, gradually changing the
ITC from being simply an information-gathering agency to
a semijudicial agency that plays an important role in determining industry-specific levels of protection. The president and the ITC are much less vulnerable to industry-
specific political pressures than the members of Congress
who had previously determined the tariff rate on each of
the thousands of items in the U.S. tariff schedule. Congress apparently decided that the time-consuming nature
of the task and the political backlash that sometimes occurred after its decisions made detailed tariff setting an
activity better left to other government units.

Under the institutional arrangements that now exist,
many trade policy actions are better explained by the set of
models emphasizing long-run self-interest or a concern for
the welfare of others than by those stressing political pressure based on short-run self-interest. The lower duty cuts
in the Tokyo and Kennedy rounds to industries characterized by a large proportion of unskilled, low-paid workers
who are generally not well organized for pressure group
purposes is an example of such an action. President Carter's veto during the Tokyo Round of a bill preventing any
duty reductions on textile and apparel products is also
difficult to account for on the basis of the pressure group
framework. Even the act of proposing protection-reducing
multilateral trade negotiations, as several presidents have
done, does not seem consistent with a short-run pressure
group view of the political process.

Many congressional actions on trade matters are also
better explained by models stressing the importance of
long-run self-interest or the pursuit of broad social and
political goals. In shaping the Trade Act of 1974, members

of the key committees undoubtedly were influenced by protectionist pressures, but an important goal seems to have been to increase the authority of Congress over the general nature of U.S. trade policy. The incident of threatening to reject the new GATT codes unless small-scale and minority U.S. business firms were given preference over foreign suppliers in government purchasing activities is explained better by a social concern framework than by a short-run pressure group model. That such legislation as the Trade Act of 1974 and the Tokyo Round codes on nontariff trade barriers was approved by Congress is also hard to account for with a short-run pressure group perspective.

The ITC's decision-making process does not appear to be explainable by either set of trade policy models. The commissioners seem to try to follow the guidelines set forth in the law without regard to pressures from the president, members of Congress, or private common interest groups. The voting pattern of the commission, however, is correlated with their political party affiliation, though less so in recent years than in the past. The guidelines in the law are sufficiently broad that commissioners holding the differing political views of the Republican and Democratic parties can differ quite legitimately in their decisions. Where there is some evidence of political pressures being exerted for the purpose of influencing the pattern of decisions is in the nomination process. Since the late 1960s Congress has sought to increase significantly the proportion of commission members with employment experience in Congress (mainly as staff personnel) and the private sector rather than in the executive branch or academe. This congressional effort is partly the result of jurisdictional disputes between the president and the Congress on trade matters and partly due to the desire by Congress for ITC decisions to reflect its more protectionist views as compared to those of the president. The evidence to date, however, does not support the hypothesis that commissioners with congressional and private sector backgrounds are more protectionist than those with executive branch or academic employment experience.

Analysis of trade policy behavior in Congress, the executive branch, and the ITC leads to the conclusion that an eclectic approach to understanding this behavior is the most appropriate one currently. Until the various models are differentiated more sharply analytically and better empirical measures for distinguishing them are obtained, it will be difficult to ascertain the relative importance of different motivations of government officials under various conditions.

In considering the trade policy behavior of public officials, several hypotheses not tied to any particular model were set forth and evaluated on the basis of historical experience. They deal mainly with comparisons between the president and Congress, as well as among groups within each of these units of government. For example, an abundance of evidence supports the hypothesis that the president tends to be more liberal on trade policy matters than the Congress. In comparing the trade policy record of the House and Senate, it is not possible to say one is more protectionist than the other; however, the Senate does seem more receptive to protectionist petitions from particular industries than the House. The time period analyzed is also consistent with the hypothesis that chairpersons of key committees with jurisdiction over trade issues have a much greater ability to assist a particular industry than the typical member of Congress. A final important conclusion supported by recent experience is that the political interactions between the president and the Congress play a major role in shaping trade legislation.

5.2 Improving the Trade Policymaking Process

Certain principles of good public policymaking and policy implementation are accepted by most individuals regardless of their personal policy preferences. Statutes, administrative directives, and other statements of policy should be workable in the sense that clear, objective standards can be applied in a consistent manner to carry out their intended purpose. Policies should be administered in an impartial, competent manner by the most appropriate government units. The implementing process should be as open and transparent as possible. Sets of policies dealing with common issues should be consistent and integrated. The purpose of this section is to evaluate selected U.S. import policies in terms of these principles.[1]

Injury Determination by the ITC

One of the key requirements for obtaining relief from either "fair" or "unfair" import competition is that there must be injury to a domestic industry. But there is considerable variation in the degree of injury required for obtaining relief from fair versus unfair competition. In the first case (the so-called escape clause provisions) the import competition must cause or threaten to cause serious injury. In cases of foreign subsidization or dumping, only material injury or the threat of material injury is required before qualifying for import relief.[2] Relief from market-disrupting imports from a communist country—another form of unfair imports under U.S. trade law—requires that the imports be "a significant cause of material injury."[3]

Section 201 of the 1974 Trade Act (the escape clause provision) provides some guidance to the ITC in distinguishing serious injury from the threat of serious injury.

The factors listed as being relevant for determining serious injury are "the significant idling of productive facilities in the industry, the inability of a significant number of firms to operate at a reasonable level of profit, and significant unemployment or underemployment within the industry."[4] In contrast, the factors cited as being relevant for determining the threat of serious injury are "a decline in sales, a higher and growing inventory, and a downward trend in production, profits, wages, or employment (or increasing underemployment) in the domestic industry concerned."[5]

As the analysis in chapter 3 of section 201 cases indicates, the ITC does not appear to follow the guidelines set forth by Congress in deciding whether there has been serious injury to a domestic industry. The economic relationships that best explain the commission's affirmative serious injury decisions are a short-run decline in profits and a longer-run fall in employment. These are variables that the ITC is directed to consider in determining the threat of serious injury rather than actual serious injury. The number of cases in which the ITC found the threat of serious injury under the 1974 criteria is too few to undertake a statistical analysis of the common economic conditions existing in these cases; however, the small number itself probably indicates the difficulty the ITC had in distinguishing the threat of serious injury from actual serious injury.

The 1974 Trade Act directs the ITC to consider such factors as the level of profits, the degree of capital utilization, and unemployment and underemployment levels in determining whether serious injury has occurred. The measure of profits used by the ITC—the ratio of net profits to sales—is not significantly related to affirmative injury decisions. Furthermore, as Adams and Dirlam point out, what is really needed is an estimate of the rate of return on investment since the ratio of profits to sales varies widely from industry to industry due to variations in capital-output ratios.[6] The ITC also does not systematically collect data on capital utilization or the degree of unemployment in an industry. For measuring the latter condition, the commission should collect information on average hours of work per employee and the number of workers laid off who still have not found a comparable job.

Clearly the ITC could improve its economic analysis in making injury determinations. In being asked to distinguish serious injury from the threat of serious injury, however, the ITC has been given an unworkable task in the sense that clear, objective standards cannot be applied in a consistent manner to discriminate between these two shades of injury. Economic investigators are not any more able to determine whether an industry not currently injured seriously is likely to be seriously injured in the future than they are able to determine future industry winners and losers in international competition.

Being threatened with serious injury should be eliminated as a condition that qualifies an industry for import relief. But the economic factors listed in section 201 for determining the threat of serious injury should be retained as relevant guidelines in determining serious injury itself. The time constraints imposed on the commission for making its report to the president and on the president for accepting or rejecting this report are sufficiently short to prevent undue hardship to an industry waiting until it is seriously injured before petitioning for import relief.

Under GATT rules on escape clause actions, if a country raises the level of protection on a product on which it had decreased protection as part of the bargaining process in a previous trade negotiation, other countries can ask for compensating duty cuts on other products. If these are not granted, they can retaliate by raising their import duties on products of export interest to the country initially raising its protective level. The unwillingness of some countries whose industries have been injured by increased import competition to undertake this compensation has led to the greater use in recent years of so-called voluntary export restraints. Under the threat that severe import restrictions will be imposed by the country with the injured industry, the countries whose increased exports have been the main cause of the injury "voluntarily" agree, outside of the GATT framework, to limit their exports of the relevant product. These actions weaken the degree of conformity to an agreed-on set of international trading rules, increase the likelihood of international economic disputes because of their discriminatory nature, and tend to bring about a more inefficient use of world resources. Furthermore, such responses as quality upgrading on the part of producers voluntarily limiting their exports and an increase in exports from suppliers in other countries tend to make this type of discriminatory action ineffective in stimulating domestic output and employment.

One proposal that might encourage countries to follow the most-favored-nation rule of the GATT is to eliminate the compensation requirement, provided protection to an injured industry is limited in duration, perhaps three to five years, and decreases over the period. The existence of serious injury itself indicates that imports have increased more rapidly than expected by the negotiating parties.

The conclusions reached concerning the difficulty of drawing the distinction between serious injury and the threat of serious injury also apply with regard to distinguishing between material injury and the threat of material injury. The section of the Trade Agreements Act of 1979 dealing with these two concepts is unworkable in the sense previously described. Therefore the threat of material injury should be dropped as a condition that qualifies an industry for import relief under U.S. laws covering "unfair" trade practices by foreign suppliers.

Obviously Congress wants the injury standard in unfair import competition cases to be easier to meet than in fair import competition cases. Given a decision by the Department of Commerce as to whether dumping has occurred or a subsidy should be countervailed, the key factors for determining material injury under the 1979 act are the effects of the dumped or subsidized imports on the domestic price and sales volume of the like product and the consequent impact of these effects on the economic condition of the domestic industry. The price and volume effects can be estimated by taking into account the margin of dumping or subsidization per unit value of imports, the ratio of imports to domestic production, the degree of substitutability between imports and domestic output, and the responsiveness of quantities demanded and supplied to changes in prices. If these price and volume estimates are significant and an examination of changes in output, market share, profits, return on investments, and utilization of capacity in the industry indicates that the industry has been injured by the dumped or subsidized imports, then a finding of material injury should be made.[7] In other words, as long as the harm caused by the imports "is not inconsequential, immaterial, or unimportant," a finding of material injury is required.[8]

The ITC does take most of the above factors into consideration in estimating the price and volume effects of the dumping or subsidization. Rather surprisingly, however, in recent years it has turned away from considering the margin of dumping or subsidization as a relevant factor.[9]

One set of circumstances that often leads to subsidization by other countries is serious injury to an industry caused by a loss of export markets. Although the problem of how to deal with seriously injured export industries has not yet arisen in the United States, it is likely to appear in the not too distant future. Just as it was proposed that other countries should not take action against temporary tariff increases designed to assist seriously injured import-competing industries, it seems reasonable for countervailing action to be waived in cases of temporary domestic subsidies to seriously injured export industries. If the subsidy does not make the industry any more competitive than before being injured, there is no material injury to others, and countervailing duties should not be imposed.

Another important issue in this area is the appropriate test to be applied by the Department of Commerce in determining if a subsidy is countervailable. The GATT subsidies code explicitly states that its signatories do not want to restrict the right of countries to use subsidies to promote desirable social and economic objectives. But the code also recognizes that some domestic subsidies can cause material injury to other countries. While neither the code nor U.S. countervailing duty law is explicit on the matter, it appears that subsidies generally available to all industries or to a particular productive factor on an equal basis should not be countervailable. The relative competitive advantage given to any one industry by a general subsidy is usually slight, while the collective effect of the subsidy tends to be offset by an appreciation of the country's currency. If a country deliberately tries to maintain an undervalued exchange rate, other countries should work through the rules of the International Monetary Fund to bring an end to this practice.

In contrast, selective subsidies aimed at particular firms or industries should be countervailable. (The ITC must find that material injury has been caused by the subsidy before countervailing duties can actually be levied.) These subsidies can provide a significant competitive edge to domestic firms and cause material injury to foreign competitors.

In deciding what subsidies are actionable under U.S. countervailing duty law, the Department of Commerce has been following guidelines based on the distinction between general versus selective subsidies.[10] It is often very difficult to draw the dividing line, however, and these guidelines have not as yet been fully tested in the courts.

An additional criterion for determining countervailable subsidies is their effect on potential real income. For example, subsidies for education and research that are available to all individuals and most industries not only meet the generality criterion but tend to raise real income in all countries. In contrast, subsidies to a particular industry that continue long after they can be justified on adjustment grounds tend to reduce real income levels for all countries.

The Substantial Cause Requirement in Section 201 Cases

Another statutory requirement for granting import relief in section 201 cases is that the increased imports must be "a substantial cause" of serious injury or threat thereof.[11] In deciding this matter, the ITC is directed to consider "an increase in imports (either actual or relative to domestic production) and a decline in the proportion of the domestic market supplied by domestic producers."[12] As noted in chapter 3, however, while the level of the import penetration ratio was nearly significant at the 10 percent level in the various regression equations estimated in trying to ascertain the economic criteria actually used by the ITC in distinguishing affirmative and negative cases of serious injury, neither the change in imports nor the change in import penetration ratios was close to being statistically significant.

The term *substantial cause* is defined in section 201 as "a cause which is important and not less than any other cause." Thus the ITC is also directed to determine whether an increase in imports or decline in domestic market share held by domestic producers is the most important cause of serious injury to an industry.

A simple analytical method for assisting in such a determination has been devised by Anne Krueger.[13] Assume that a downward trend in an industry's employment level is a reasonable indicator of possible serious injury. As Krueger points out, the rate of change of employment in an industry is definitionally equal to the sum of three components: the rate of growth of domestic consumption, the growth rate of the share of domestic output in consumption, and (minus) the rate of growth of labor productivity. The second of these components is the same as one of the criteria mentioned in section 201 (the proportion of the domestic market supplied by domestic producers), except that it includes exports in the numerator. Thus the ratio can fall if exports decline as well as if imports increase.[14]

In dividing employment changes in U.S. manufacturing industries between 1970 and 1976 into the three components, Krueger found that a decline in the ratio of production to domestic consumption generally was not the most important factor "accounting for" a decline in an industry's employment level. Decreases in consumption or increases in labor productivity were the dominant factors. The relative size of the components does not imply their causal importance, however, since two-way causal importance relationships can be imagined among all the variables. For example, increases in productivity or imports can, by lowering prices, cause increases in consumption. Or though productivity gains might statistically account for most of the employment displacement in an industry, the rise in productivity may be a response to greater import competition or changes in factor prices.[15] Nevertheless, the

Krueger analysis is a useful starting place from which to investigate causality in a particular industry.

Table 5.1 indicates the results of applying the technique to ITC cases between 1975 and 1979. The analysis confirms Krueger's findings that market growth and changes in labor productivity were generally more important than shifts in trade in accounting for changes in employment. In only eleven of the twenty-seven cases in which employment declined was the trade factor the largest of the negative components. Employment declined in sixteen of nineteen cases in which the commission decided that some form of import relief was warranted. If the commission's finding of injury in these industries is accepted and the Krueger technique is used for determining if the necessary condition for import relief is satisfied—that imports are not less important than any other cause contributing to the employment loss—the result is that relief is justified in ten of the sixteen cases. In six of the seven decisions in which the commission rejected import relief on the grounds that imports were not a substantial cause of injury, the Krueger technique supports the ITC's determination.[16] Nevertheless, the Krueger analysis is but a useful first survey of the issue as to whether imports are a substantial cause of serious injury.

Another important issue concerning the substantial cause requirement has arisen. In explaining their negative finding in the 1980 automobile case, some of the commissioners on the majority side argued that the recession was a more important cause of serious injury in the industry than increased imports.[17] In their affirmative decision in the 1983 stainless steel case, however, all the commissioners declined to regard the fall in steel consumption associated with the recession as a single cause and found increased imports to be a more important cause of serious injury than any other cause.

Table 5.1
Contribution of domestic demand, trade, and labor productivity to rate of employment change, 1975–79 (continuous percentage rates)

ITC decision	Industry	Domestic demand	Production consumption ratio	Labor productivity	Employment
Negative	Birch plywood door skins	-10.36	19.55	-40.51	-31.32
Negative	Bolts, nuts, and large screws of iron or steel	5.85	-2.57	-5.16	-1.88
Negative	Small screws	7.03	0.03	-4.21	2.85
Negative	Wrapper tobacco	-13.86	6.27	-7.31	-14.90
Negative	Asparagus	-2.04	-0.95	-1.53	-4.52
Negative	Stainless steel and alloy tool steel	14.25	2.45	-11.98	4.71
Negative	Slide fasteners and parts thereof	-0.12	-1.18	-3.30	-4.59
Affirmative	Footwear	-2.85	-2.55	0.80	-4.60
Affirmative	Stainless steel table flatware	-3.70	-0.30	1.83	-2.17
Negative	Certain gloves	3.32	-0.49	-0.87	1.96
Affirmative	Mushrooms	10.07	-0.88	-14.24	-5.04
Affirmative	Ferrocyanide and ferrocyanide pigments (iron blue pigment)	-4.31	-2.45	-2.49	-9.24
Affirmative	Shrimp	0.20	-3.46	0.00	-3.26
Negative	Round stainless steel wire	-3.63	1.66	3.64	-1.65
Affirmative	Honey	4.29	-4.41	0.34	0.22
Affirmative	Sugar	-2.96	4.80	0.23	2.07
Negative	Mushrooms	7.52	-0.17	-16.23	-8.88
Affirmative	Footwear	-3.55	-2.96	1.39	-5.11

Affirmative	Television receivers	3.27	-2.54	-11.01	-10.28
Affirmative	Low-carbon ferrochromium	-11.42	-11.75	6.49	-16.67
Negative	Cast-Iron cooking ware	11.47	-12.57	1.96	-3.06
Negative	Fresh cut flowers	4.21	-1.30	-1.47	1.44
Negative	Certain headwear	21.72	-4.29	-6.63	10.81
Negative	Cast-iron stoves	26.08	-23.25	-1.89	0.93
Negative	Live cattle and certain edible meat products of cattle	3.72	0.29	-4.33	-0.31
Negative	Malleable cast-iron pipe and tube fittings	-5.90	0.70	-0.48	-5.68
Affirmative	Bolts, nuts, and large screws of iron or steel	-2.66	-3.64	-0.05	-6.35
Affirmative	High-carbon ferrochromium	9.60	-8.85	-2.09	-1.34
Affirmative	Citizen band (CB) radio transceivers	74.77	-18.67	-25.73	30.37
Affirmative	Certain stainless steel flatware	5.09	-12.76	1.90	-5.77
Negative	Unalloyed, unwrought zinc	-3.92	-3.08	3.58	-3.43
Affirmative	Unalloyed, unwrought copper	-1.65	-3.91	1.44	-4.12
Negative	Fishing rods	9.15	-7.15	-1.08	0.92
Negative	Fishing reels	0.22	-3.20	5.82	2.84
Affirmative	Artificial baits and flies	10.89	-8.04	-4.81	-1.95
Affirmative	High-carbon ferrochromium	0.15	-8.33	1.52	-6.66
Affirmative	Clothespins	0.34	-6.91	3.99	-2.58
Affirmative	Bolts, nuts, and large screws of iron or steel	-3.50	-2.69	-0.84	-7.03

Note: The employment change in each industry is over the four-year period preceding the ITC decision. Production and consumption are measured in physical units. Labor productivity is employment divided by output, with no correction for capacity utilization or part-time workers.

Source: Reports issued by the International Trade Commission on 201 import relief cases.

As Commissioner Paula Stern argued in the automobile case, "It is unlikely that Congress intended to make relief more difficult to obtain for industries beset by repetitive cyclical downturns."[18] The history of the escape clause provision suggests that Congress and the president have been concerned with ascertaining the relative importance of causes of injury that affect no more than a relatively small number of sectors at any one time rather than with all causes of injury, including short-term macroeconomic factors that can adversely affect many industries at the same time. As Stern points out, if all causes of injury are considered, no industry is likely to qualify for import relief in a severe recession, since the aggregate decline in income at that time will tend to be a more important cause of injury than a concurrent increase in imports due to some factor that affects a comparatively small number of products. Increases in imports brought about by macroeconomic conditions, such as a rapid cyclical appreciation of the U.S. dollar, can cause serious injury to many import-competing (and export) industries and should also be excluded in comparing causes of injury. If currency appreciations are not excluded as a qualifying cause for import relief, then the widespread increase in protection that otherwise could be justified would be regarded by other countries as a beggar-thy-neighbor policy. The sequence of retaliatory increases in protection that might be started could endanger the existing world trading regime. Furthermore, since the dollar may well depreciate rapidly as macroeconomic conditions change whereas any protection given under section 201 lasts for at least five years, the policy of granting protection under these conditions can bring about a protection-induced expansion of import-competing sectors that turns out to be excessive under more normal exchange-rate conditions.

Since the intent of section 201 and its counterpart in the

General Agreement on Tariffs and Trade (GATT), Article 19, is to provide selective import relief because of microeconomic causes of injury, the wording of this section should be modified to exclude short-term macroeconomic causes of import injury. Under this framework the ITC would first estimate the injurious impact of macroeconomic factors on such variables as employment, capacity utilization, and profits and then exclude these effects from the total decrease in each of these variables. If the remaining decline in these variables was sufficient to be regarded as serious injury, the relative importance of the various micro-related causes of this injury would be compared in the usual manner. Isolating the import impact of changes in macroeconomic variables is not an easy task, but since commissioners presently estimate the relative importance of the different factors causing serious injury to an industry to determine if import increases are as important as any other cause, this effort could be integrated easily into the current process of injury determination.

Relationships between the President,
the Congress, and the ITC

A major theme of this study is that it is not possible to understand the manner in which U.S. trade policy is formed without analyzing the interactions among the president, the Congress, and the ITC on trade issues. Since these interactions are so important in shaping trade policy, every effort should be made to ensure that the formally established relationships among these units of government are open and consistent with each other and also facilitate the achievement of the objectives for which they were established. This section suggests several modifications in the existing relationships motivated by these principles of good policymaking.

Under present procedures by which an industry obtains import relief under the so-called escape clause provisions of the 1974 Trade Act, the ITC only considers whether increased imports of an article cause serious injury or the threat thereof to a domestic industry producing a similar article. If an affirmative decision is reached, this determination, along with the commission's finding on the amount of increased protection needed to remedy the injury, is sent to the president. The president must provide import relief unless he determines that such relief "is not in the national economic interest of the United States."[19] In deciding this issue, the president is directed to take into account, in addition to other considerations he may deem relevant, such factors as the probable effectiveness of import relief in promoting adjustment, the effect of import relief on consumers and on the degree of competition in domestic markets, the impact on other industries of any required compensatory cuts in protection for other sectors, and the economic costs of not granting protection on the directly affected workers and on the communities in which they reside.[20]

The manner in which the analysis of these factors is carried out and reported by the executive branch does not meet the standards of good public policymaking. In particular, the analyses are neither undertaken in a consistent manner nor the results of the investigations made available to the major participants and the public in general. An interagency committee, chaired by the Office of the U.S. Trade Representative (USTR) and composed of individuals from such departments as Commerce, Labor, State, Treasury, and Agriculture, carries out the study (usually with one agency being assigned the responsibility for preparing the basic paper) and then makes a recommendation to the president as to whether he should accept or reject the ITC affirmative decision and the import relief recommended by this organization. The personnel involved in the analyses frequently change, and the quality of the analyses varies considerably.

Most objectionable about the procedures followed is that—in contrast to ITC injury determinations—the basic facts and relationships on which the interagency committee relies in making its recommendation are not made available to the public or the petitioning industry. Furthermore in reporting his decision, the president usually explains his reasoning in only general terms. As a consequence of this procedure, both those favoring and those opposing import relief in a particular case tend to believe that unjustifiable political factors rather than sound economic reasoning determined the outcome of the case. This reaction undermines the confidence of the participants and the general public in the fairness of the entire import relief process under sections 201–203 of the Trade Act of 1974.

This process could be improved in two alternative ways. One is for the president to explain his reasoning in more detail and to include in his report the basic data on which he and the interagency committee relied in reaching a conclusion. This is what the ITC does in making its recommendations on section 201 cases. The commissioners, either individually or in groups, usually explain how relevant economic facts support their conclusion. Furthermore, each report includes extensive statistical tables presenting information on such economic conditions as profit levels, wages, imports and import penetration ratios, prices, employment, and so forth. The president should do the same with respect to the economic factors relevant to his decision, including the likely increase in the prices of the relevant products as a consequence of protection and the impact of this on consumers and producers who use the items as inputs into their productive processes, the likely effects on the industry and its workers if protection is granted as well as if it is not granted, the likely effect of any compensatory cuts required, and the likely impact of protection on the market structure of the industry.

The Senate version of the Trade and Tariff Act of 1984 did include a provision that would further the goal of greater openness, but it was rejected by the House-Senate conference committee. Specifically the Senate bill required ITC recommendations to the president for some form of import restrictions also to be submitted to the Council of Economic Advisers (CEA) for analysis. Within thirty days the CEA would have to make a report to the president and Congress on the effects of the ITC's recommendations on prices, on revenues, on employment in the industry seeking protection, on consumers and on other industries, on the U.S. balance of payments, and on U.S. competitiveness.

An alternative way of providing the needed openness in the procedures for determining whether import relief is in the national interest is to direct the ITC to analyze the impact of its recommended import relief in terms of the various factors specified in the law. The ITC already collects many of the statistics needed for such an evaluation and has a staff of economists and industry specialists who are trained to carry out such an analysis. Furthermore as required by law, the ITC undertakes investigations similar to the one proposed here in advising the president at the outset of a trade negotiation as to the probable economic effect of the modification of import duties on items under consideration for duty cuts.

The report to the president from the ITC would consist of two parts. The first would be the same as the present report on injury determination, and the second would analyze the various factors relevant for the president to make a decision on national interest grounds. The commission members would not themselves vote on this issue, but each would be free to present his or her own analysis of these factors. The president would make the final decision, using the analysis of the ITC, as well as any other analysis within the executive branch that he wanted. The publication by the ITC of all the facts and relationships relevant for deciding if an industry has been seriously injured and if import relief is in the national interest is likely to improve the quality of the decision-making process in the executive branch and increase the degree of confidence of the participants and general public in the entire set of import relief procedures.

Bringing the ITC into the decision-making process in all section 301 cases would also improve the implementation of U.S. trade laws. Under the present law USTR makes the determination as to whether the policy of a foreign government "is inconsistent with the provision of . . . any trade agreement" or "is unjustifiable, unreasonable, or discriminatory and burdens or restricts United States commerce," after holding public hearings and seeking advice from the private sector.[21] The president may also request the views of the ITC concerning the probable impact on the U.S. economy of any action he is considering against the foreign government.

USTR does not possess sufficient staff or expertise to make the determinations it is charged with under section 301. An impartial, semijudiciary agency such as the ITC, with its considerable staff expertise, is better able to make these factual determinations. As in section 201 cases the ITC, in addition to reporting fully on the reasons for its decision, should recommend a particular retaliatory action to the president if it makes an affirmative decision. Furthermore the ITC should assess the probable economic impact of their recommended action on the United States. As in import injury cases, however, the president should not be required to accept the decision or recommended counteraction by the ITC. But the increased openness associated with the formal involvement of the ITC in section 301 cases will increase the confidence of the major participants and the general public in the fairness and competency of those involved in this decision-making process. The suggested changes also have the merit of making the procedures for handling section 201 and section 301 cases more consistent with each other. An alternative to increasing ITC involvement in 301 cases would be to require USTR to make the kind of detailed reports in these cases that the ITC makes in section 201 cases.

Changes in antidumping and countervailing duty procedures are also needed on grounds of "good" public policymaking. Under the present statutes, the Executive Office of the President (through USTR) is not directly involved in either antidumping or countervailing duty cases. The Commerce Department determines whether dumping or actionable subsidization has occurred, and the ITC determines whether the affected industry has suffered material injury. If both agencies make affirmative findings, an antidumping or countervailing duty must be levied automatically.

In fact, in major cases, USTR is often actively involved in working out solutions mutually agreeable to the domestic and foreign sectors that do not involve the imposition of extra duties. The 1982 antidumping and countervailing duty petitions covering carbon steel products from seven European Community members and South Africa, Brazil, Rumania, and Spain illustrate this point. The volume of trade covered by the affirmative findings of Commerce and the ITC was so large that imposing extra duties through normal administrative channels could have touched off retaliatory actions with serious foreign policy consequences. The cases had to be handled at the presidential level where a mutually satisfactory agreement involving temporary quotas was eventually worked out. Interventions of this sort, however, undermine the confidence of the participants and general public in the fairness of antidumping and countervailing duty procedures. Consequently the statutes should be changed to give USTR a specified amount of time, perhaps sixty to ninety days, after the final determinations by Commerce and the ITC to work out acceptable solutions aimed at eliminating the dumping and subsidization or at least mitigating the distorting and protective effects of these activities and the increased duties to which they lead.

Certain modifications in the relationships between the Congress and the ITC also are necessary to improve the implementation of U.S. trade laws. Although Senator Long and his colleagues were probably correct in believing that the president had too much influence on the ITC during the 1950s and 1960s, the balance of influence over the ITC between the president and Congress has now shifted too far in favor of Congress. The recent proclivity on the part of Congress to accept as commissioners only individuals with employment experience as staff members in Congress does not seem consistent with the goal of choosing ITC members who will implement the law in an independent, competent manner. Thus far no evidence indicates that such individuals have been unduly influenced in their decisions by congressional pressures. To avoid even the appearance of such a possibility, commission members should have diverse backgrounds of employment experience. Section 172 of the Trade Act of 1974, which deals with the organization of the commission, should be amended to state that the commission should be composed of individuals representative of diverse employment backgrounds.

Another change that would help to balance the influence of Congress and the president on the commission is to restore the pre-1974 budgeting process for the ITC. The Trade Act of 1974 requires the president to include the commission's proposed annual appropriation in the budget without revision. Under normal budgetary procedures, first the president and then the Congress can affect the magnitude of an agency's budget. To remove the influence of the president entirely would seem to shift the balance of political influence too much in favor of Congress.

The most important set of intragovernmental relationships affecting the nature of trade policy is that between the president and the Congress. Much of trade policy history over the last fifty years can be interpreted as a continuing effort by Congress to establish relationships with the president that free Congress from detailed policymaking yet ensure that its general intent on trade matters is followed. The procedures worked out between the Congress and the president in formulating the Trade Act of 1974 and in implementing the agreements reached in the ensuing multilateral trade negotiation did much to meet these dual congressional objectives and are likely to be followed in future trade initiatives.[22]

The congressional–executive branch relationships fashioned during this period demonstrate very clearly that the president does not simply propose legislation and the Congress dispose of it. The executive branch and the Congress worked together closely in drafting the various provisions of the 1974 Trade Act. This act also provided for direct participation in the Tokyo Round negotiations by members and staff of the House Ways and Means and Senate Finance Committees. But the most important new procedures developed were those dealing with the manner in which the agreements reached on nontariff measures would be implemented. The president was required to submit a bill to Congress approving any such agreements and proposing any needed changes in U.S. law to implement them. Furthermore, prior to concluding any agreement and before submitting the bill to Congress, the president was directed under the 1974 Trade Act to consult with the House Ways and Means and Senate Finance committees, as well as with every other congressional committee having jurisdiction over the matters covered. Once submitted, however, there could not be any amendments to the agreements or the bill implementing them.

Under the arrangements agreed on for carrying out these various procedures, the president, through USTR, submitted detailed legislative proposals to the House Ways and Means and Senate Finance committees for review in informal, closed-door sessions. These two committees not only handled the process of consultation with other relevant committees but took the lead role in drafting the implementing legislation. They operated, however, within the terms of the agreements on nontariff measures that the executive branch had reached with its negotiating partners. Under these arrangements the president was able to obtain congressional approval of the new GATT codes quite easily, and Congress was able to affect the nature of U.S. trade policy in a substantive manner by specifying the procedures for implementing the codes under U.S. law.

Most of the individuals closely involved in establishing and then working within the Tokyo Round procedures regard them as a highly successful compromise that brought a new spirit of cooperation between Congress and the executive branch and yet permitted each government unit to pursue its somewhat different policy goals. If this cooperative attitude can be maintained in future trade negotiations, the institutional arrangements developed in the

Tokyo Round will be favorably compared with those that were established in the Trade Agreements Act of 1934 and in the subsequent reciprocal trade negotiations.

One possibly troublesome point in the future is the requirement that the president consult with every congressional committee with jurisdiction over matters affected by a trade agreement. The increased complexity of trade negotiations, as they have changed from tariff-reducing exercises to highly technical negotiations on a wide range of nontariff measures, has led to a diffusion of committee jurisdiction over trade matters.[23] In the future some congressional committees may not be so willing to allow the House Ways and Means and the Senate Finance committees to take the lead roles in directing trade legislation through the Congress. This could bring about jurisdictional disputes that hamper the implementation of trade agreements; however, the manner in which the Trade and Tariff Act of 1984 was passed suggests that this will not be a serious problem. The Ways and Means and Finance committees took the lead in putting the bill in final form, but members of the Committee on Energy and Commerce and the Committee on Foreign Affairs were included on the House-Senate conference committee for the purpose of considering certain parts of the bill.

Outside of periods of formulating trade legislation or negotiating trade agreements, probably the most important congressional means for influencing trade policy until recently has been the power to override the president's negative decisions on particular import injury cases. If the president rejected an affirmative import-relief decision by the ITC, the Congress, by a majority in both houses of those present and voting, could impose the relief recommended by the ITC. In the *Chadha* decision of 1983, however, the Supreme Court declared such congressional veto provisions unconstitutional on the grounds that they violated the constitutional doctrine of separation of powers. While Congress has never actually vetoed a negative presidential import-injury decision, the threat of doing so in particular cases seems to have led to actions by the president to help an industry in ways other than an increase in protection on a most-favored-nation basis. In the Trade and Tariff Act of 1984, Congress changed this disapproval provision so that it would conform to the *Chadha* decision by substituting joint resolutions of disapproval that can be vetoed by the president for concurrent resolutions not subject to presidential veto. This clearly represents some weakening in the power of Congress in relation to that of the president, but it is not likely to have much effect on the basic nature of trade policy because of the many other ways in which Congress can exert pressure on the president.

Notes

Chapter 1

1. The best-known historical study along these lines is F. W. Taussig, *The Tariff History of the United States* (Cambridge: Harvard University Press, 1931).

2. The absence of market-distorting conditions such as external economies and retaliatory behavior on the part of trading partners is assumed in deriving this result.

3. Two outstanding studies by noneconomists of the manner in which trade policies are determined are E. E. Schattschneider, *Politics, Pressures and the Tariff* (Englewood Cliffs, N.J.: Prentice-Hall, 1935), and R. A. Bauer, I. Pool, and L. A. Dexter, *American Business and Public Policy: The Politics of Foreign Trade*, 2d ed. (Chicago: Aldine-Atherton, 1972).

4. Dennis C. Mueller, "Public Choice: A Survey," *Journal of Economic Literature* 14 (June 1976): 395–433. For a recent collection of essays on this topic, see David C. Colander (ed.), *Neoclassical Political Economy: The Analysis of Rent-Seeking and DUP Activities* (Cambridge, Mass.: Ballinger Publishing Company, 1984).

5. The courts, which also sometimes play an important policy role in trade matters, are not analyzed in this study.

6. It is also necessary to assume that the share of income that any consumer spends on a commodity at a given set of relative commodity prices does not change as the individual's income changes. For a more detailed discussion of the public choice

model than is set forth below, see Baldwin (1976) and Frey (1984). Mayer (1984) develops a formal model of endogenous tariff formation based on the approach used here.

7. For a full discussion of the welfare implication of free trade versus import protection, see P. A. Samuelson, "The Gains from Trade Once Again," *Economic Journal* 72 (December 1962): 820–829, and Robert E. Baldwin, "The New Welfare Economics and Gains in International Trade," *Quarterly Journal of Economics* 66 (February 1952): 91–101.

8. The tie-in must be such that if free trade is selected, a nondistorting tax is levied on the gainers (whether they vote or not) and the proceeds redistributed to a particular set of individuals who will lose under a policy of free trade unless they receive this compensation.

9. More specifically the government cannot discriminate among consumers by requiring some to pay an import duty on an item while allowing others to import the identical good without paying the duty.

10. It is also assumed that their net gains are sufficient to compensate the losers (that is, the capitalists). If voting costs for workers exceed their gains under free trade while the voting costs for capitalists fall short of their gains under the tariff situation, workers will not vote, and the tariff policy will be selected. Under these conditions, however, one cannot say that the free trade outcome is in fact potentially welfare superior to the tariff policy.

11. Unlike the perfect-information and no-voting-costs assumptions, dropping the assumption that income can be redistributed in a costless fashion does not lead to welfare-inferior outcomes, provided the costs of compensating are included in the tax levied on all gainers. If voting costs are absent, there will still be no incentive for the gainers not to vote since they will pay their share of the redistribution costs whether they vote or not.

12. Mayhew (1974) exemplifies a political scientist who believes that the desire to be reelected is the main consideration influencing congressional behavior.

13. For an analysis of the short-run income distribution effects of tariffs, see M. Mussa, "Tariffs and the Distribution of Income: The Importance of Factor Specificity, Substitutability, and Intensity in the Short and Long Run," *Journal of Political Economy* 82

(December 1974): 1191–1203, and Robert E. Baldwin, "Rent-Seeking and Trade Policy: An Industry Approach," *Weltwirtschaftliches Archiv* (Review of World Economics) 120 (1984), 662–677.

14. Olson points out, however, that even if an industry does not meet these criteria, it may succeed in organizing if it produces a private good, such as a journal that provides useful technical information to its members, and collects funds for lobbying by selling this good.

15. According to the common interest group model, the failure of consumers to form effective lobbying groups to oppose protection is due to their large numbers and to the comparatively small adverse income effect that they perceive protecting any particular product usually has on them. The comparatively small adverse impact on most export industries of granting protection to any particular import-competing industry is cited as a reason why effective counterlobbying by export-oriented industries does not usually occur. However, using a game-theoretic approach, some writers, for example, Brock and Magee (1978) and Findlay and Wellisz (1982) have developed endogenous tariff models in which a strong pro-tariff group and a strong pro-free trade group compete against each other in the tariff-determining process.

16. In terms of the theories developed by political scientists to explain public policy formation, both the Olson and Caves models are examples of a pure version of pluralism in which the role of government officials and government institutions is minimized.

17. The recent studies by Nordlinger and others represent a return by some political scientists to a more statist approach to political leadership. See Krasner (1982); Skocpol (1982).

18. See Nordlinger (1981) for a listing of the various means the state can use to offset and diffuse opposition.

19. Oleszek (1978), p. 24.

20. Fenno (1973), p. 84.

21. See Manley (1970), pp. 288–291, and Pastor (1980), pp. 162–163.

22. Kenneth J. Arrow, "Gifts and Exchange," in E. S. Phelps, ed., *Altruism, Morality, and Economic Theory* (New York: Russell Sage Foundation, 1975).

23. If the individual's welfare increases, the relationship is one of envy rather than altruism.

24. Arrow, "Gifts and Exchange," p. 17. Arrow is discussing the reasons why people give blood to help individuals they do not personally know.

25. See W. M. Corden, *Trade Policy and Economic Welfare* (Oxford: Clarendon Press), 1974, pp. 320–321; James H. Cassing, "Alternatives to Protectionism" in J. Levenson and J. W. Wheeler, eds., *Western Economies in Transition* (Boulder, Colo.: Westview Press, 1980), pp. 396–397; and Jonathan Eaton and Gene M. Grossman, "Tariffs as Insurance: Optimal Commercial Policy When Domestic Markets Are Incomplete," *Canadian Journal of Economics* (forthcoming).

26. Phelps, *Altruism*, p. 2.

27. Corden, *Trade Policy*, p. 107.

28. Conybeare (1984) uses a game-theoretic approach to analyze the bargaining among countries on tariff levels during trade wars. For an excellent survey of the burst of recent literature analyzing national levels of protection within a bargaining framework, see Gene M. Grossman and J. David Richardson, "Strategic Trade Policy: A Survey of Issues and Early Analysis," Princeton University, International Finance Section, Special Papers in International Economics, No. 15, April 1985.

29. The view of public policy formation on which the hegemonic model rests is one that stresses both the importance of collective goals and autonomous behavior by government officials.

30. There is general agreement that the model performs better in accounting for trade policy shifts in the early post–World War II period than in recent years.

31. See Baldwin (1984) for an analysis of shifts in post–World War II U.S. trade policy.

Chapter 2

1. U.S. Constitution, Art. 1, sec. 8. Congress is, however, prohibited from imposing export taxes. See U.S. Constitution, Art. 1, sec. 10.

2. Peter Buck Feller and Ann Carlisle Wilson, "United States Tariff and Trade Law: Constitutional Sources and Constraints," *Law and Policy in International Business* 8, no. 1 (1976): 107.

3. The ability of Congress to delegate its trade policy powers has also been tested in the courts. See ibid., pp. 109–111.

4. For a brief history of the countervailing duty law, see Robert V. Guido and Michael F. Morone, "The Michelin Decision: A Possible New Direction for U.S. Countervailing Duty Law," *Law and Policy in International Business* 6, no. 1 (Winter 1974): 241–242.

5. See Anti-Dumping Act of 1921, 67th Cong., 1st sess., 1921, ch. 14, tit. II, as well as the earlier effort to deal with dumping as a form of unfair competition in the Revenue Act of 1916, 64th Cong., 1st sess., ch. 463, tit. VIII, sec. 801. See also Tariff Act of 1922, 67th Cong., 2d sess., ch. 356, secs. 316 and 317.

6. Trade Agreements Act of 1934, 73d Cong., 2d sess., 1921, ch. 474, sec. 350.

7. The view expressed many years ago by Senator Arthur Vandenberg concerning detailed tariff rate making on the part of Congress is still widely held by members of both the House and Senate. In describing this process as an "atrocity," he stated that "it lacks any element of economic science or validity. I suspect that 10 members of the Senate, including myself, who struggled through the 11 months it took to write the last congressional tariff act, would join me in resigning before they would be willing to tackle another general congressional tariff revision." Quoted in William B. Kelly, Jr., ed., *Studies in United States Commercial Policy* (Chapel Hill: University of North Carolina Press, 1963), p. 78.

8. Frederick M. Kaiser, "Congressional Control of Executive Actions: Alternatives to the Legislative Veto," Report No. 83-227 GOV (Congressional Research Service, December 27, 1983), p. 5. This report discusses various ways, other than the congressional veto, that Congress can use to control executive actions.

9. In response to the restructuring directive, the president shifted the responsibility for administering the antidumping and countervailing duty laws as well as the provisions relating to protection for national security purposes from the Treasury Department to the Commerce Department.

10. See Raymond J. Ahearn and Alfred Reifman, "Trade Policy-making in the Congress," in R. E. Baldwin, ed., *Recent Issues and Initiatives in U.S. Trade Policy* Conference Report (Cambridge, Mass.: National Bureau of Economic Research, 1984).

11. An exception may be an export industry that itself is being accused of causing injury abroad and thus is a likely candidate for retaliation.

12. The importance of gaining influence within Congress as a goal of legislators is stressed by Richard F. Fenno, Jr., *Congressmen in Committees* (Boston: Little, Brown, 1973).

13. For a discussion of procedural differences between the House and Senate, see Walter J. Oleszek, *Congressional Procedures and the Policy Process* (Washington, D.C.: Congressional Quarterly Press, 1978).

14. In his message to Congress on the administration's bill, President Nixon stated that these items would be excluded from the scheme, but he did not make this part of the bill.

15. For an analysis of this episode, see Paula Stern, *Water's Edge: Domestic Politics and the Making of American Foreign Policy* (Westport, Conn.: Greenwood Press, 1979).

16. This section is based in part on an earlier pamphlet by Robert E. Baldwin, "The Political Economy of Postwar U.S. Trade Policy," *Bulletin*, 1976-4, New York University, Graduate School of Business Administration, New York, 1976.

17. Democrats and Republicans favoring the bill numbered 112 and 160, respectively.

18. For some industries in some counties, employment data were not given in *County Business Patterns* because of disclosure problems. In most of these cases, it was possible to make a reasonable estimate by taking the midpoint of the employment size classes that were given in the tables. When employment in a particular industry was in the open-ended size class of 500 or more, a figure was determined either by subtracting the sum of all other industries from an appropriate subtotal for manufacturing or by utilizing the employment size classes given by the state for reporting units of 500 or more employees. Combining counties into congressional districts also required the use of rough estimating tech-

niques since counties are often not coterminous with congressional districts. Use of the tables in the *Congressional District Data Book* listing the division of cities into various congressional districts was helpful in allocating employment in a particular county into more than one congressional district.

19. The unions included are the International Brotherhood of Electrical Workers of America, the Communications Workers of America, and the United Steelworkers of America, all actively opposed to the bill. The precise variable used was the contributions of these unions in 1974 to House members who voted for or against the trade bill in 1973 and who chose to run for office again in 1974. Presumably these 1974 contributions were highly correlated with the aid given by the unions in earlier periods. The information on contributions was obtained from records on file at the National Information Center on Political Finance (Citizens' Research Foundation), Washington, D.C.

20. The third equation, which divided the industries more finely, was omitted because the log of the likelihood function failed to approach zero smoothly.

21. See U.S. Congress, Senate, *Congressional Record*, October 12, 1978, p. 518552.

22. For an analysis of this lobbying incident, see Ward Sinclair, "Congress' Last Hours: A Big Bazaar," *Washington Post*, October 20, 1978; and U.S. Congress, Senate, *Congressional Record*, October 12, 1978, pp. 518550-69.

23. *Washington Post*, February 22, 1979.

24. *Administration Textile Program*, White House, February 15, 1979.

25. U.S. Congress, House, *Congressional Record—Extension of Remarks*, May 21, 1979, p. E-2413.

26. The agreements were initialed by the various deputies rather than those representatives with ministerial rank, since several details in the tariff package had to be worked out and formal U.S. acceptance could occur only after Congress had approved the nontariff agreements. A formal signing ceremony was planned for the fall. For an analysis of the various agreements, see Robert E. Baldwin, *The Multilateral Trade Negotiations: Towards Greater*

Liberalization? (Washington, D.C.: American Enterprise Institute, 1979).

27. Prior to this, a finding that other countries were subsidizing products exported to this country was sufficient for the imposition of a countervailing duty.

28. At the time, the Steel Caucus had 135 members in the House and 38 in the Senate.

29. Trade Agreements Act of 1979, Public Law 96-39, 96th Cong., sec. 771, 93 Stat. 177-78.

30. Trade Agreements Act of 1979, sec. 771, 93 Stat. 178.

31. The same provision but with respect to injury determinations by the commission in dumping cases had been introduced into the law in 1958.

Chapter 3

1. The commission was known as the Tariff Commission until 1975.

2. Quoted in John M. Dobson, *Two Centuries of Tariffs: The Background and Emergence of the U.S. International Trade Commission* (Washington, D.C.: Government Printing Office, 1976), p. 87.

3. Revenue Act of 1916, 64th Cong., 1st sess., ch. 463, sec. 702, 704.

4. Ibid., sec. 703. This responsibility to conduct investigations for the president and Congress still exists.

5. Upon a finding that a 50 percent tariff increase would be insufficient to equalize the costs of production, the president could direct that a duty be levied on the American selling price (ASP) of a similar article produced in this country. Moreover, the law directed that this ASP method of valuation must be followed for coal tar products.

6. Tariff Act of 1922, 67th Cong., 2d sess., ch. 356, sec. 316, 317.

7. For a discussion of the criticisms of the commission, see Dobson, *Two Centuries of Tariffs*, pp. 97–102.

8. Tariff Act of 1930, 71st Cong., 2d sess., ch. 497, sec. 337, 338.

9. Ibid., sec. 336. Another change was that the president's option to impose additional duties in instances of unfair import practices was eliminated; he could only either completely exclude foreign imports or take no action at all.

10. Tariff Act of 1930, ch. 497, sec. 336.

11. William B. Kelly, Jr., ed., *Studies in United States Commercial Policy* (Chapel Hill: University of North Carolina Press, 1963), p. 125.

12. Ibid., p. 127.

13. Trade Agreements Extension Act of 1951, ch. 141, sec. 7.

14. Trade Expansion Act of 1962, Public Law 87-794, October 11, 1963, sec. 252, 76 Stat. 879.

15. Eligibility requirements for adjustment assistance to workers in the form of readjustment allowances, retraining programs, and job search allowances, as well as for firms in the form of technical and financial assistance, were eased even more, but the determination of eligibility of workers and firms for assistance was taken away from the ITC and turned over to the secretary of labor and secretary of commerce, respectively. The Trade and Tariff Act of 1984 also eased the criteria for injury determination somewhat.

16. Trade Agreements Act of 1979, Public Law 96-39, July 26, 1979, sec. 701.93, Stat. 151. A material injury test is applied only if the exporting country is a signatory of the GATT subsidies code, if imports are duty free, or if a bilateral agreement covering this matter has been negotiated with the country.

17. These figures and the ones on final determinations are from the U.S. International Trade Commission, *Operation of the Trade Agreements Program, 32nd Report–35th Report* (Washington, D.C.: Government Printing Office, 1982–1984).

18. However, in response to an affirmative determination by the commission, the president can impose import restrictions only against those countries that are the source of the disruptive imports.

19. Public Law 95-106, August 17, 1977, 91 Stat. 867. However, the president cannot select either of the two most recent appointees as chairperson or a person of the same party as the immediately preceding chairperson.

20. See Eugene T. Rossides, *U.S. Customs, Tariffs, and Trade* (Washington, D.C.: Bureau of National Affairs, 1977), pp. 521–532, and Stanley D. Metzger and Alfred G. Mursey, "Judicial Review and Tariff Commission Actions and Proceedings," *Cornell Law Review* 56 (January 1971): 285–341.

21. Revenue Act of 1916, 64th Cong., 1st sess., sec. 700.

22. One writer who earlier called attention to the partisan nature of voting on escape clause cases is William B. Kelly, Jr., "The Expanded Trade Agreements Escape Clause, 1955–61," *Journal of Political Economy* 70, no. 1 (February 1962): 37–63.

23. The chi-square values for a test of this hypothesis are 21.46, 15.90, and 3.43 for the periods 1949–1962, 1963–1973, and 1974–1983, respectively.

24. U.S. Congress, House, Committee on Ways and Means, *Comparison of Ratios of Imports to Apparent Consumption, 1968–72*, prepared by the staff of the U.S. Tariff Commission (Washington, D.C.: Government Printing Office, 1973).

25. U.S. Congress, Senate, *Hearing before the Committee on Finance*, September 28, 1967, p. 18.

26. Senator Long explained the various actions of the committee at this time in the nomination hearings for Commissioners Leonard and Newsom. See ibid., October 9, 1968.

27. Ibid., October 14, 1977.

28. Ibid., June 23, 1971.

29. Ibid., June 23, 1971. During these nomination hearings, Senator Long declared that during the earlier period he had "blocked the Democratic or Republican appointees until we could have some understanding that the Commission was going to regain its independence as I saw it" (p. 26).

30. Ibid., October 14, 1977.

31. One of the individuals who was linked to a particular manufacturing sector always disqualified himself in cases dealing with this industry.

32. For a statement of the less rigid standards followed by some commissioners, see "Additional Statement by Commissioners

Thunberg and Clubb," in *Report to the President on Eyeglass Frames*, Tariff Commission Report 219 (Washington, D.C., October 1967).

33. Prior to the 1962 act, the law stated that increased imports resulted "in whole or in part" from a tariff concession, but the commission had long presumed that greater imports were at least in part related to tariff concessions. See supplementary statement of Chairman Metzger, *Report to the President on Barbers' Chairs*, Tariff Commission Publication 228 (Washington, D.C., January 1968), p. 9.

34. Trade Act of 1974, Public Law 93-618, sec. 201, 88 Stat. 2012.

35. Ibid.

36. Ibid.

37. Ibid.

38. There is some evidence of a change over the ten-year period in the explanatory power of the variables reflecting the short-run change in profits, the longer-run change in employment, and the interaction of these two variables. During the period 1974–1979, when thirty-seven cases were decided by the commission, these three variables were significant at the 10 percent level or lower in all five equations shown in table 3.3. Furthermore in contrast to the entire period (or the 1980–1983 period by itself), the profit-change and employment-change variables were generally significant at a lower level than the dummy variable indicating whether these two variables were both negative.

39. This hypothesis is suggested by ex-commissioner Penelope Thunberg in "Tales of a Onetime Commissioner," *Challenge* (July–August 1977).

40. Irving B. Kravis, "The Trade Agreements Escape Clause," *American Economic Review* 44, no. 3 (June 1954): 319–338.

41. Dean A. Peterson, "The Escape Clause: A Critical Analysis" (master's thesis, George Washington University, 1966).

42. Charles Pearson, "Adjusting to Imports of Manufactures from Developing Countries" (paper prepared for a seminar at the Washington Center of Foreign Policy Research, February 8, 1979).

43. Ibid.

Chapter 4

1. Part of this chapter was presented at the Eleventh Pacific Trade and Development Conference on Trade and Growth of the Advanced and Developing Countries in the New International Economic Order, Seoul, Korea, September 1–4, 1980. See Wontack Hong and Lawrence B. Krause (1981).

2. The president was not required to accept the limits set by the commission, but if he did not, he had to report his reasons to Congress.

3. Trade Expansion Act of 1962, Public Law 87-794, sec. 221b, 76 Stat. 875.

4. Ibid., sec. 252.

5. The 1974 Trade Act (sec. 301a, 88 Stat. 2041) gave the president the authority to impose import restrictions if other countries introduced "unjustifiable or unreasonable restrictions on access to supplies of food, raw materials, or manufactured or semimanufactured products which burden or restrict United States commerce."

6. The language in the 1979 act is similar to the 1962 law and simply directs the president to take appropriate steps against a foreign action that is "unjustifiable, unreasonable, or discriminatory, and burdens or restricts United States commerce."

7. Trade Agreements Act of 1955, Public Law 86, chap. 169, sec. 7b, 69 Stat. 166.

8. See Trade Agreements Act of 1979, Public Law 96-39, Title X, 93 Stat. 300-07, and Stanley D. Metzger and Alfred G. Mursey, "Judicial Review of Tariff Commission Actions and Proceedings," *Cornell Law Review* 52 (January 1971): 290. Under section 22 of the Agricultural Adjustment Act, the ITC, at the request of the president, determines whether agricultural products are being imported in such quantities as to render or tend to render ineffective the Department of Agriculture's price-support programs.

9. Trade Act of 1974, sec. 250.

10. A president's own policy preferences depend in large part on his previous education and employment experience.

11. See J. M. Finger, H. Keith Hall, and Douglas R. Nelson, "The Political Economy of Administered Protection," *American Economic Review* 72, no. 3 (June 1982): 452–466 for a detailed discussion of these two different means of securing protection.

12. Trade Act of 1974, sec. 202a, 88 Stat. 2014.

13. The ITC variable also was not significant, either alone or in combination with any of the other variables tried.

14. Steel shipments increased only 1.9 percent in 1977, whereas increases ranging from 7 percent to 12 percent had been predicted, and industrial production in general rose 5.6 percent. Similarly employment in the steel industry dropped 0.4 percent compared to a rise of 3.7 percent for total nonagricultural employment. See American Iron and Steel Institute, *Annual Statistical Report* (Washington, D.C., 1977), and *Economic Report of the President* (January 1979). For a detailed analysis of the industry's economic difficulties as well as of the effects of the trigger price mechanism, see Robert W. Crandall, *The Steel Industry in Recurrent Crisis* (Washington: The Brookings Institution, 1981).

15. Ibid.

16. Industry leaders also mentioned required capital expenditures for pollution control facilities as a source of their difficulties. These jumped from about $250 million annually in the early 1970s to over $500 million in 1977.

17. Trade Act of 1974, sec. 321, 88 Stat. 2046.

18. In fact, average employment in the industry fell from 454,000 in 1976 to 452,000 in 1977 and the total hours worked from 876.7 million hours to 875.9 million hours. American Iron and Steel Institute, *Annual Statistical Report*, 1977.

19. Allegheny Ludlum Steel, Armco Steel, and six other companies filed charges of both unfair import practices under section 337 and dumping under the 1921 antidumping law in the case of certain welded stainless steel pipe and tube; the American Iron and Steel Institute claimed under section 301 that a bilateral agreement between Japan and the European Community diverted steel from Japan into the U.S. market; Armco filed subsidization charges against silicon steel from Italy under the countervailing duty law. The ITC issued a cease-and-desist order

under section 337, but this was disapproved by the president. The Treasury decided that the same products were also being dumped, but the ITC made a negative determination on injury. In the countervailing duty case, Treasury came up with a negative decision on the subsidy issue. No action was taken in the section 301 market diversion case, but it may have had some effect on the decision in early 1978 to continue the quota on specialty steel.

20. New York Times, September 22, 1977.

21. Ibid., September 30, 1977.

22. Ibid., October 1, 1977.

23. Ibid., October 12, 1977.

24. Hugh Patrick and Hideo Sato, "The Political Economy of United States-Japan Trade in Steel" in Cozo Yamamura, ed., *Policy and Trade Issues of the Japanese Economy* (Seattle: University of Washington Press, 1982).

25. Since the president was not permitted under the law to cut more than 60 percent, the formula became a linear one of 60 percent for the United States above a duty level of 21 percent (the lowest rate at which the formula yields a cut of 60 percent).

26. This "effective protection" concept assumes fixed prices of goods used as intermediate inputs.

27. In order to utilize the data bank of industry characteristics assembled by the staff of the ITC, the tariff cuts were grouped into a slightly modified form of the pure SIC, as developed by commission staff.

28. Letting t_i^0 and t_i^1 be, respectively, the initial tariff rate and the actual new tariff rate offered on any item; M_i^0 the 1976 value of imports for that item; and n the number of TSUS items in a particular industry, the first cut equals

$$(1) \quad \text{Cut 1} = \frac{\sum_1^n (t_i^0 M_i^0 - t_i^1 M_i^0)}{\sum_1^n (t_i^0 M_i^0)} \; ;$$

and the second cut equals

$$(3) \quad \text{Cut 2} = \frac{\sum_{1}^{n} \left[M_i^o \left(\left\{ t_i^o \left[1 - \left(\frac{t_i^o}{t_i^o + .14} \right) \right] \right\} - t_i^1 \right) \right]}{\sum_{1}^{n} M_i^o}.$$

29. U.S. International Trade Commission, Office of Economic Research, *The U.S. International Trade Commission's Industrial Characteristics and Trade Performance Databank* (Washington, D.C., June 1975).

30. The total capital stock of an industry was also introduced as an independent variable to determine if financial size mattered in deciding upon tariff cuts. It turned out to be insignificant.

31. The simple correlation coefficient between the average tariff reduction and the average tariff level is $+.19$.

32. There were 119 industries (out of 262) in which at least 5 percent of the tariff line items were not reduced at all in the Kennedy Round.

33. The list of the two-, three-, and four-digit SIC industries opposing passage of the act is given in table 2.1. Textiles and apparel (SIC 22 and 23) and rubber tires (SIC 301) were added to this list.

34. PAY 76 and LQ 76 (not shown) are also significant if either is substituted for SKUNSK.

35. See Robert E. Baldwin and R. Spence Hilton, "A Technique for Indicating Comparative Costs and Predicting Changes in Trade Ratios," *Review of Economics and Statistics* 66, no. 1 (February 1984): 105–110.

Chapter 5

1. The evaluation and suggestions for improvement are undertaken within a framework that accepts the intended purposes of existing trade policies, as well as the general institutional structure for implementing these policies. The proposed changes aim at improving the implementation of these policies. For a broader evaluation of U.S. trade policies by the author, see Robert E. Baldwin and T. Scott Thompson, "Responding to Trade-

Distorting Policies of Other Countries," *American Economic Review, Papers and Proceedings* 74, no. 2 (May 1984): 271–276.

2. Trade Agreements Act of 1979, Public Law 96-39, sec. 771, 93 Stat. 178. Countervailing or antidumping duties can also be imposed if the establishment of an industry in the United States is materially retarded.

3. Trade Act of 1974, Public Law 93-618, sec. 406, 88 Stat. 2063.

4. Ibid., sec. 201, 88 Stat. 2012. It is explicitly stated that the determination of both serious injury and the threat of such injury need not be based only on the factors listed.

5. Ibid.

6. Walter Adams and Joel B. Dirlam, "Import Competition and the Trade Act of 1974: A Case Study of Section 201 and its Interpretation by the International Trade Commission," *Indiana Law Journal* 52 (Spring 1977): 46.

7. Trade Agreements Act of 1979, sec. 771, 93 Stat. 178.

8. Ibid.

9. Walter Adams and Joel B. Dirlam, "The Trade Laws and Their Enforcement by the International Trade Commission," in R. E. Baldwin, ed., *Recent Issues and Initiatives in U.S. Trade Policy*, Conference Report (Cambridge, Mass.: National Bureau of Economic Research, 1984).

10. Shannon Stock Shuman and Charles O. Verrill, Jr., "Recent Developments in Countervailing Duty Law and Practice," in Baldwin, *Recent Issues*.

11. Trade Act of 1974, sec. 201, 88 Stat. 2012.

12. Ibid.

13. Anne O. Krueger, "Impact of Foreign Trade on Employment in United States Industry," in *Current Issues in Commercial Policy and Diplomacy*, eds. John Black and Brian Hindley (London: Macmillan, 1980), p. 77.

14. Usually U.S. industries in which imports are increasing rapidly and employment is declining are not major exporters.

15. See Gene M. Grossman, "Comment," in *Import Competition*

and Response, ed. Jagdish Bhagwati (Chicago: University of Chicago, 1982), pp. 397–398.

16. These negative cases were: birch plywood door skins; wrapper tobacco; slide fasteners; stainless steel wire; low-carbon ferrochromium; live cattle; and unwrought zinc. The one among these seven where the trade factor was more important (though only marginally so) than either the domestic demand or productivity factor in contributing to the employment decline was low-carbon ferrochromium.

17. *Certain Motor Vehicles and Certain Chassis and Bodies Thereof,* Inv. No. TA-201-44, USITC Publication 1110 (December 1980).

18. Ibid., p. 129.

19. Trade Act of 1974, sec. 202, 88 Stat. 2014.

20. Ibid.

21. Trade Agreements Act of 1979, sec. 901, 93 Stat. 245.

22. For a detailed analysis of these procedures, see I. M. Destler and Thomas R. Graham, "United States Congress and the Tokyo Round: Lessons of a Success Story," *World Economy* 3, no. 1 (June 1980): 53–70.

23. See Raymond J. Ahearn and Alfred Reifman, "Trade Policymaking in the Congress," in Baldwin, *Recent Issues,* for further discussion of this diffusion of power.

Bibliography

Adams, Walter, and Joel B. Dirlam. 1977. "Import Competition and the Trade Act of 1974: A Case Study of Section 201 and Its Interpretation by the International Trade Commission." *Indiana Law Journal* 52, no. 3 (Spring): 535–599.

Adams, Walter, and Joel B. Dirlam. 1984. "The Trade Laws and Their Enforcement by the International Trade Commission." In R. E. Baldwin, ed., *Recent Issues and Initiatives in U.S. Trade Policy.* Cambridge, Mass.: National Bureau of Economic Research.

Ahearn, Raymond J., and Alfred Reifman. 1984. "Trade Policymaking in the Congress." In R. E. Baldwin, ed., *Recent Issues and Initiatives in U.S. Trade Policy.* Cambridge, Mass.: National Bureau of Economic Research.

American Iron and Steel Institute. 1977. *Annual Statistical Report.* Washington, D.C.: American Iron and Steel Institute.

Arrow, Kenneth J. 1975. "Gifts and Exchange." In E. S. Phelps, ed., *Altruism, Morality, and Economic Theory.* New York: Russell Sage Foundation.

Baldwin, Robert E. 1952. "The New Welfare Economics and the Gains from Trade." *Quarterly Journal of Economics* 66:91–101.

Baldwin, Robert E. 1976. "The Political Economy of Postwar U.S. Trade Policy." *Bulletin,* 1976-4. New York: New York Graduate School of Business.

Baldwin, Robert E. 1979. *The Multilateral Trade Negotiations: Towards Greater Liberalization?* Washington, D.C.: American Enterprise Institute.

Baldwin, Robert E. 1984. "The Changing Nature of U.S. Trade Policy since World War II." In R. E. Baldwin and A. O. Krueger, eds., *The Structure and Evolution of Recent U.S. Trade Policy.* Chicago: University of Chicago Press.

Baldwin, Robert E. 1984. "Rent-Seeking and Trade Policy: An Industry Approach." *Weltwirtschaftliches Archiv* (Review of World Economics) 120, no. 4:662–677.

Baldwin, Robert E., and T. Scott Thompson. 1984. "Responding to Trade-Distorting Policies of Other Countries." *American Economic Review, Papers and Proceedings* 74, no. 2:271–276.

Baldwin, Robert E., and R. Spence Hilton. 1984. "A Technique for Indicating Comparative Costs and Predicting Changes in Trade Ratios." *Review of Economics and Statistics* 66, 1:105–110.

Bale, Malcolm D. 1977. "United States Concessions in the Kennedy Round and Short-Run Adjustment Costs: Further Evidence." *Journal of International Economics* 2:145–148.

Ball, D. S. 1967. "United States Effective Tariffs and Labor's Share." *Journal of Political Economy* 75:183–187.

Bauer, R. A., I. Pool, and L. A. Dexter. 1972. *American Business and Public Policy: The Politics of Foreign Trade.* 2d ed. Chicago: Aldine-Atherton.

Bhagwati, Jagdish N. 1982. "Directly Unproductive Profit-Seeking (DUP) Activities." *Journal of Political Economy* 90:988–1002.

Bhagwati, Jagdish N., ed. 1982. *Import Competition and Response.* Chicago: University of Chicago Press.

Bhagwati, Jagdish N., and T. N. Srinivasan. 1980. "Revenue-Seeking: A Generalization of the Theory of Tariffs." *Journal of Political Economy* 88:1069–1087.

Brock, W. A., and S. P. Magee. 1978. "The Economics of Special Interest Politics." *American Economic Review* 68, no. 2 (May): 246–250.

Cassing, James H. 1980. "Alternatives to Protectionism." In J. Levenson and J. W. Wheeler, eds., *Western Economies in Transition.* Boulder: Westview Press.

Cassing, James, Timothy J. McKeown, and Jack Ochs. 1984. "A Theory of the Political Economy of Protection." Department of Economics, University of Pittsburgh, Working Paper No. 169.

Caves, R. E. 1976. "Economic Models of Political Choice: Canada's Tariff Structure." *Canadian Journal of Economics* 9, no. 2 (May): 278–300.

Cheh, J. H. 1974. "United States Concessions in the Kennedy Round and Short-Run Labor Adjustment Costs." *Journal of International Economics* 4:323–340.

Cohen, Stephen D., and Ronald I. Meltzer. 1982. *United States International Economic Policy in Action.* New York: Praeger Publishers.

Colander, David C., ed. 1984. *Neoclassical Political Economy: The Analysis of Rent-Seeking and DUP Activities.* Cambridge, Mass.: Ballinger Publishing Company.

Constantopoulos, M. 1974. "Labour Protection in Western Europe." *European Economic Review* 5:313–318.

Conybeare, John. 1984. "National Tariff Levels: Theory and Evidence on Bargaining During Trade Wars." Presented at meeting of American Economic Association, December 28–30. Dallas, Texas.

Corden, W. M. 1974. *Trade Policy and Economic Welfare.* Oxford: Clarendon Press.

Crandall, Robert W. 1981. *The Steel Industry in Recurrent Crisis.* Washington: The Brookings Institution.

Destler, I. M., and Thomas R. Graham. 1980. "United States Congress and the Tokyo Round: Lesson of a Success Story." *World Economy* 3, no. 1:53–70.

Dobson, John M. 1976. *Two Centuries of Tariffs: The Background and Emergence of the U.S. International Trade Commission.* Washington, D.C.: Government Printing Office.

Eaton, Jonathan, and G. M. Grossman. 1985. "Tariffs as Insurance: Optimal Commercial Policy When Domestic Markets Are Incomplete." *Canadian Journal of Economics* 18, no. 2 (May):258–272.

Feller, Peter B., and Ann C. Wilson. 1976. "United States Tariff and Trade Law: Constitutional Sources and Constraints." *Law and Policy in International Business* 8:105–123.

Fenno, Richard F., Jr. 1973. *Congressmen in Committees.* Boston: Little, Brown.

Fenno, Richard F., Jr. 1978. *Home Style: House Members in Their Districts.* Boston: Little, Brown.

Fieleke, N. 1976. "The Tariff Structure for Manufacturing Industries in the United States: A Test of Some Traditional Explanations." *Columbia Journal of World Business* 11, no. 4 (Winter): 98–104.

Findlay, Ronald, and S. Wellisz. 1982. "Endogenous Tariffs, the Political Economy of Trade Restrictions, and Welfare." In J. Bhagwati, ed., *Import Competition and Response.* Chicago: University of Chicago Press.

Finger, J. M., H. Keith Hall, and Douglas R. Nelson. 1982. "The Political Economy of Administered Protection." *American Economic Review* 72, no. 3:452–466.

Fiorina, Morris P. 1974. *Representatives, Roll Calls, and Constituencies.* Lexington, Mass.: Lexington Books.

Frey, Bruno S. 1984. *International Political Economics.* Oxford: Basil Blackwell.

Froman, Lewis A., Jr. 1963. *Congressmen and Their Constituents.* Chicago: Rand McNally and Company.

Grossman, Gene M. 1982. "Comment," in J. Bhagwati, ed., *Import Competition and Response.* Chicago: University of Chicago Press.

Grossman, Gene M., and J. David Richardson. 1985. "Strategic Trade Policy: A Survey of Issues and Early Analysis." Special Papers in International Economics, no. 15. Princeton: Princeton University, International Finance Section.

Guido, Robert V., and Michael F. Morone. 1974. "The Michelin Decision: A Possible New Direction for U.S. Countervailing Duty Law." *Law and Policy in International Business* 6, no. 1:241–242.

Helleiner, G. K. 1977. "The Political Economy of Canada's Tariff Structure: An Alternative Model." *Canadian Journal of Economics* 4, no. 2 (May): 318–326.

Hong, Wontack, and Lawrence B. Krause, eds. 1981. *Trade and Growth of the Advanced Developing Countries in the Pacific Basin.* Seoul: Korea Development Institute.

Johnson, Harry G. 1960. "The Cost of Protection and the Scientific Tariff." *Journal of Political Economy* 68, no. 4 (August): 327–345.

Kaiser, Frederick M. 1983. "Congressional Control of Executive Actions: Alternatives to the Legislative Veto." Congressional Research Service Report No. 83-227 GOV, December 27.

Kau, James B., and Paul Rubin. 1982. *Congressmen, Constituents, and Contributors.* Boston: Martinus Nijhoff Publishing.

Kelly, William B., Jr. 1962. "The Expanded Trade Agreements Escape Clause, 1955–61." *Journal of Political Economy* 70, no. 1:37–63.

Kelly, William B., Jr., ed. 1963. *Studies in United States Commercial Policy.* Chapel Hill: University of North Carolina Press.

Keohane, Robert O. 1984. *After Hegemony: Cooperation and Discord in the World Political Economy.* Princeton: Princeton University Press.

Kindleberger, Charles P. 1973. *The World Depression, 1929–1939.* Berkeley: University of California Press.

Kingdon, John W. 1973. *Congressmen's Voting Decisions.* New York: Harper and Row.

Krasner, Stephen D. 1976. "State Power and the Structure of International Trade." *World Politics* 28 (April): 317–347.

Krasner, Stephen D. 1978. *Defending the National Interest: Raw Materials, Investments and U.S. Foreign Policy.* Princeton: Princeton University Press.

Krasner, Stephen D. 1982. "Approaches to the State: Alternative Conceptions and Historical Analysis." Stanford: Department of Political Science, Stanford University.

Krauss, M. B. 1978. *The New Protectionism: The Welfare State and International Trade.* New York: New York University Press.

Krueger, Anne O. 1974. "The Political Economy of the Rent-Seeking Society." *American Economic Review* 64:291–303.

Krueger, Anne O. 1980. "Impact of Foreign Trade on Employment in United States Industry." In J. Black and B. Hindley, eds., *Current Issues in Commercial Policy and Diplomacy*. London: Macmillan.

Lavergne, R. P. 1983. *The Political Economy of U.S. Tariffs: An Empirical Analysis*. New York: Academic Press.

Manley, John F. 1970. *The Politics of Finance: The House Committee on Ways and Means*. Boston: Little, Brown.

Mathews, David, and James Stimson. 1975. *Yeas and Nays: Normal Decision Making in the U.S. House of Representatives*. New York: John Wiley and Sons.

Mayer, W. 1984. "Endogenous Tariff Formation." *American Economic Review* 74 (December): 970–985.

Mayhew, David R. 1974. *Congress: The Electoral Connection*. New Haven: Yale University Press.

Metzger, Stanley, and Alfred G. Mursey. 1971. "Judicial Review of Tariff Commission Actions and Proceedings." *Cornell Law Review* 56, no. 2 (January): 285–341.

Mueller, Dennis C. 1976. "Public Choice: A Survey." *Journal of Economic Literature* 14 (June): 395–433.

Mussa, M. 1974. "Tariffs and the Distribution of Income: The Importance of Factor Specificity, Substitutability, and Intensity in the Short and Long Run." *Journal of Political Economy* 82 (December): 1191–1203.

Neustadt, Richard E. 1976. *Presidential Power: The Politics of Leadership with Reflections on Johnson and Nixon*. New York: John Wiley and Sons.

Niskanen, William A. 1971. *Bureaucracy and Representative Government*. Hawthorne, New York: Aldine.

Nordlinger, Eric. 1981. *On the Autonomy of the Democratic State*. Cambridge, Mass.: Harvard University Press.

Nowzad, B. 1978. *The Rise of Protectionism*. Washington, D.C.: International Monetary Fund.

Oleszek, Walter J. 1978. *Congressional Procedures and the Policy Process*. Washington, D.C.: Congressional Quarterly Press.

Olson, Mancur. 1965. *The Logic of Collective Action: Public Goods and the Theory of Groups.* Cambridge, Mass.: Harvard University Press.

Olson, Mancur. 1983. "The Political Economy of Comparative Growth Rates." In D. C. Mueller, ed. *The Political Economy of Growth.* New Haven: Yale University Press.

Pastor, Robert A. 1980. *Congress and the Politics of U.S. Foreign Economic Policy, 1929–1976.* Berkeley: University of California Press.

Patrick, Hugh, and Hideo Sato. 1982. "The Political Economy of United States-Japan Trade in Steel." In Cozo Yamamura, ed., *Policy and Trade Issues of the Japanese Economy* (Seattle: University of Washington Press, 1982).

Pearson, Charles. 1979. "Adjusting to Imports of Manufactures from Developing Countries." Paper presented at a seminar at the Washington Center of Foreign Policy Research, Washington, D.C., February 8.

Peltzman, S. 1976. "Toward a More General Theory of Regulation." *Journal of Law and Economics* 19:211–248.

Peterson, Dean A. 1966. "The Escape Clause: A Critical Analysis." Master's thesis, George Washington University.

Phelps, E. S., ed. 1975. *Altruism, Morality, and Economic Theory.* New York: Russell Sage Foundation.

Pincus, J. 1975. "Pressure Groups and the Pattern of Tariffs." *Journal of Political Economy* 83 (August): 757–778.

Samuelson, P. A. 1962. "The Gains from Trade Once Again." *Economic Journal* 72 (December): 820–829.

Schattschneider, E. E. 1935. *Politics, Pressures, and the Tariff.* Englewood Cliffs, N.J.: Prentice-Hall.

Shuman, Shannon S., and Charles O. Verrill, Jr. 1984. "Recent Developments in Countervailing Duty Law and Practice." In R. E. Baldwin, ed., *Recent Issues and Initiatives in U.S. Trade Policy.* Cambridge, Mass.: National Bureau of Economic Research.

Sinclair, Ward. 1978. "Congress' Last Hours: A Big Bazaar." *Washington Post,* October 20.

Skocpol, Theda. 1982. "Bringing the State Back In: False Leads and Promising Starts in Current Theories and Research," presented at a conference on States and Social Structure at the Seven Springs Conference Center, Mount Kisco, New York, February 25–27.

Stern, Paula. 1979. *Water's Edge: Domestic Politics and the Making of American Foreign Policy.* Westport, Conn.: Greenwood Press.

Stigler, George J. 1974. "Free Riders and Collective Action: An Appendix to Theories of Economic Regulation." *Bell Journal of Economics and Management Science* 5, no. 2:359–365.

Stigler, George J. 1975. "The Economic Theory of Regulation." In *The Citizen and the State.* Chicago: University of Chicago Press.

Takacs, W. E. 1981. "Pressures for Protectionism." *Economic Inquiry* 19 (October): 687–693.

Taussig, F. W. 1931. *The Tariff History of the United States.* Cambridge, Mass.: Harvard University Press.

Thunberg, Penelope. 1977. "Tales of a Onetime Commissioner" *Challenge* (July–August).

U.S. Congress. Anti-Dumping Act of 1921. 1921. 67th Congress, session 1, Chapter 14, May 27.

U.S. Congress. House. 1979. *Congressional Record—Extension of Remarks.* May 21.

U.S. Congress. House. Committee on Ways and Means. 1973. *Comparison of Ratios of Imports to Apparent Consumption, 1968–72.* Washington, D.C.: Government Printing Office.

U.S. Congress. Public Law 96-39. 96th Congress, Trade Agreements Act of 1979.

U.S. Congress. 1975. Public Law 93-618. Trade Act of 1974, January 3.

U.S. Congress. 1955. Public Law 86. Chapter 169, Trade Agreements Extension Act of 1955, June 21.

U.S. Congress. 1962. Public Law 87-794. 87th Congress, Trade Expansion Act of 1962, October 11.

U.S. Congress. 1975. Public Law 93-618. 93d Congress, Trade Act of 1974, January 3.

U.S. Congress. 1916. Revenue Act of 1916. 64th Congress, session 1, Chapter 463, Title 7, September 8.

U.S. Congress. Senate. 1965. Hearing before the Committee on Finance. October 9.

U.S. Congress. Senate. 1971. Hearing before the Committee on Finance. June 23.

U.S. Congress. Senate. 1977. Hearing before the Committee on Finance. October 14.

U.S. Congress. Senate. 1978. *Congressional Record,* October 12.

U.S. Congress. Tariff Act of 1922. 67th Congress, session 2.

U.S. Congress. Trade Agreements Act of 1934. 73d Congress, session 2, Chapter 475, June 12, 1934.

U.S. International Trade Commission. Office of Economic Research. 1975. *The U.S. International Trade Commission's Industrial Characteristics and Trade Performance Databank.* Washington, D.C.: International Trade Commission.

U.S. International Trade Commission. 1980. *Certain Motor Vehicles and Certain Chassis and Bodies Thereof.* TA-201-44, USITC Publication 1110. Washington, D.C.: International Trade Commission.

U.S. International Trade Commission. 1982–1984. *Operation of the Trade Agreements Program, 32nd Report–35th Report.* Washington, D.C.: International Trade Commission.

U.S. Tariff Commission. 1967. *Report to the President on Eyeglass Frames.* Tariff Commission Publication 219. Washington, D.C.: Tariff Commission.

U.S. Tariff Commission. 1968. *Report to the President on Barbers' Chairs.* Tariff Commission Publication 228. Washington, D.C.: Tariff Commission.

Washington Post. 1979. February 22.

White House. 1979. Administration Textile Program, February 15.

Index